SMILES OF GOD

SMILES OF GOD

The Flowers of
St Thérèse of Lisieux

Felicity Leng

BURNS & OATES
A Continuum imprint
LONDON • NEW YORK

Burns & Oates
A Continuum imprint
The Tower Building   15 East 26th Street
11 York Road   New York
London SE1 7NX   NY 10010

www.continuumbooks.com

First published 2003

British Library Cataloguing-in-Publication Data
A catalogue record for this book is available from the British Library.

ISBN 0–86012–349–9 (paperback)

Typeset by RefineCatch Limited, Bungay, Suffolk
Printed and bound by Cromwell Press Ltd, Trowbridge, Wiltshire

A flower offers nectar: it is morning's daughter, springtime's charm, the source of perfumes, the grace of young women, the love of poets: it is as short-lived as humankind yet leaves its petals for us as it passes . . . The first Christians decked their martyrs' bodies and their altars in the catacombs with flowers, and we put them in our churches to recall those actions. In the secular world their colours stand for our emotions, their greenness for hope, their whiteness for innocence, their roseate hues for modesty. Whole nations view flowers as the interpreters of their feelings. They are books we long to read, and they never mislead us, for the only revolutions their transient narratives relate are the movements of the human heart.

François-René de Chateaubriand

If a little flower could talk, I think it would say quite simply what God had done for it, and not hide any of his gifts. It wouldn't say, in mock humility, that it wasn't pretty and didn't smell sweet, that the sun had withered its petals or a storm bruised its stem, if it knew all that wasn't true.

St Thérèse of Lisieux

Contents

List of Illustrations

Acknowledgements

Quotations from the Bible are taken for the most part from the Revised Standard Version © 1973 by the Division of Christian Education of the National Council of the Churches of Christ in the United States of America, used with permission. Where it is necessary to approximate to the French versions used by Thérèse, RSV or NRSV has been adapted minimally and the Authorized Version, the Douay/Rheims translation and *The New Testament in Modern English* by J. B. Philips (London, 1960) have been drawn on for certain words and phrases.

Quotations from *The Story of a Soul* and certain other texts of Thérèse's works as well as some testimonies have been taken and adapted from the translations of *L'Histoire d'une Âme* by T. N. Taylor published by and copyright © Burns & Oates 1912, 1926, 1947, and are used with the permission of the Continuum Publishing Company Ltd, as are quotations from the *Collected Works of St John of the Cross*, tr. E. Allison Peers, copyright © Burns & Oates 1935, 1953, *Introduction to the Devout Life*, tr. A. Ross, copyright © Burns & Oates 1924, and *The Imitation of Christ*, tr. R. A. Knox and M. Oakley, copyright © Evelyn Waugh and Michael Oakley 1959. Quotations from Thérèse's Letters have been taken from the translation of the *Collected Letters of St Thérèse* by F. N. Sheed, copyright © Sheed & Ward 1949, and are used with the permission of the Continuum Publishing Company Ltd.

Illustrations are reproduced from the author's drawings. That of the saxifrage on p. 70 is based, with the artist's permission, on one in *Drawings of British Plants* by Stella Ross-Craig (London, 1957–9).

Introduction:
The Flowering of St Thérèse

Creation is but a single thought in a thousand forms, and comparison is the art or instinct by which we search this divine language of universal analogies to find more ways of expressing things . . . the language of images, the mysterious links between worlds invisible and visible.

Alphonse de Lamartine

God sometimes communicates himself to us in a blazing light, at other times gently, veiled in symbols and imagery.

Thérèse of Lisieux

'A flower is a smile of God.' In a short dramatic piece for Christmas Day 1894, Thérèse Martin, by then in her fourth year as Sister Thérèse of the Holy Child and the Holy Face at the Carmelite convent in Lisieux, attributed these words to an angel of the Child Jesus:

> A flower is a smile of God,
> A distant echo of heaven,
> A single, fleeting note
> Of God's own music,
> A perfectly-formed note

In his all-making harmony,
A voice full of mystery, dear Saviour,
That sings of your great power:
    Infinitely melodious,
    Sweetly harmonious
Silence of flowers,
Telling of God in his grandeur.

These flowers that we love so,
Jesus, I know, are your friends,
For you come from heavenly meadows
To find your sisters, the flowers.
Holy Child, I know you are eager
To gather our fragrant souls.
Dear Jesus, Lily of the valley,
There is nothing you would not give
For one of us, your flowers.
    Mystery beyond words,
    Word of words, our Beloved,
You must weep still
As you take up your harvest of flowers.[1]

The image of God smiling in his flowers is simple and immediately comprehensible, yet grounded in Scripture and devotional tradition. It is as nuanced and profound as many more intricate utterances of learned mystics and spiritual writers. The immediate (though far from sole) inspiration for the theme of Thérèse's playlet was a retreat Father Lemonnier gave at the Lisieux Carmel in October 1894. He recommended constant offering to Jesus of the 'roses of our love' on behalf of sinners, and as a means of sharing in his sacrifice. Then, he said, a Carmelite would become a 'little flower' whom Jesus would 'come one day to gather to himself'.[2] Thérèse took the notion of the human soul as a flower, with all its scriptural, devotional and literary associations, and completed the metaphor with an image that marks it with her own special charm and originality. It is one of the most revealing of the large number of expressions in her works that put us in touch with her sensibility.

The recurrent word-pictures in Thérèse's autobiography, letters, poems, plays, prayers and commentaries bring to life the more than century-old sepia photographs of the saint. More effectively than the usual invocations, statues or stained-glass representations of Thérèse, her metaphors evoke not only the landscape and gardens of her childhood and the garden of a Carmelite convent in provincial France but the scenery of her mind, soul and emotions. They encapsulate her observations on her walks and journeys of experience and imagination, and supply the dimension of the real Thérèse missing from the plate photographs in which she is frozen as child and adolescent, professed nun and sacred actress, and seems so appealing but as often solemn and even enigmatic.

Thérèse was a feeling person as well as a creative mind, and her written works are more affective than abstract. They approach the condition of art, especially poetry, and like all worthwhile art and poetry rely on imagery characteristic of the artist-poet's psyche and vocation. Of all the image-clusters in the writings and recorded talk of the Little Flower, those that evoke not only the flowers of her native Normandy but the others she glimpsed and gathered in the expanses of her spiritual adventure are the most expressive. By focusing on this aspect of what Thérèse wrote and said, I have tried to disclose more clearly one of the major yet neglected ways in which we can commune with the personality of this most varied woman.

* * *

In the English-speaking world St Thérèse of Lisieux is known, almost invariably, as 'the Little Flower'. The mawkish associations of this sobriquet have dissuaded me, and I am sure many others, from more appropriate acquaintance with and study of her life and works. When I read her 'Springtime story of a little white Flower' ('Histoire printanière d'une petite Fleur blanche . . .', the autobiography dedicated to Mother Agnes of Jesus – her sister Pauline) and her letters, I was able to discard the 'ludicrous distortions and all those crystallized roses'[3] – the verbal clichés and intentionally misleading portraits that have deformed her image. As I came to appreciate the relevance of her evocations of gardens, roses and lilies, and especially those of insignificant wild flowers, I found that I was more, not less, captivated by 'God's little flower', as she called herself and her message.

The real physical appearance of Thérèse[4] in her sister Céline's original untouched photographs (fully accessible only since 1961) has gradually, even if far from entirely, replaced her sugary, sentimental image in a vast number of books, drawings, statues and other aids to devotion. Similarly, I believe, an interpretative account of Thérèse's use of flower imagery in her writings and conversation, and of relevant aspects of the traditions and circumstances that prompted them, will reinforce her presence as a transforming inspiration in many people's lives. It will also help them in their search for spiritual enlightenment in the twenty-first century, and even dispose them to respect the natural world more effectively.

To see Thérèse in a less sentimental light and understand her importance does not mean screening out the roses of her infancy, and of her poems, plays and 'pious recreations'.[5] It means seeing and understanding them in the interactive contexts of her life, reading, listening and creative imagination, 'to the scandal and trial of every sort of fanatic, even of those who would like to turn the Church into an austere and lugubrious cemetery, instead of a garden in bloom'.[6]

Nature, and flowers in particular, real and symbolic, played an important part not only in Thérèse's short life but after her death. The occasions range all the way from a neighbour's prophetic poem written on the eve of Thérèse's birth, ending with the line 'You will be a rose one day,' to the fulfilment, in various ways, of her prophecy that she would send a shower of roses on earth after her death. Thérèse's own physical, mental and spiritual development was like a flower that takes root, grows and blossoms in the sunshine, sheds its petals and dies. In essence, that is how she records her struggle to become a whole, unique person within the far from wholly self-imposed constraints of her epoch, of petit-bourgeois life in the provinces, of an increasingly defensive Church in the era of the Third Republic, and of women's role in society then.

Thérèse's 'little way' led from her early childhood experiences, through her attempts to overcome scruples and an over-sensitive nature, and her role as a teacher of postulants, to her varied, and continuing, inspiration of ordinary people searching in this life for fulfilment through love, and striving for perfection by 'being what he wants us to be', and therefore by openness to God's will acting in and through them.

Thérèse's helping, healing function was recognized soon after her death, and in 1997 she was formally declared to be a 'Doctor of the Church' (thus fulfilling her school chaplain's unwitting prophecy in addressing her as 'My little Doctor of the Law!' (when she was ten). 'Doctor' in this sense means teacher, and puts her in the same category as such formidable intellects as Augustine, Bernard and Thomas Aquinas. But the term has always included an element of 'thaumaturgy', in the sense of curative miracle-working, and is increasingly interpreted in the sense of 'healer'. As early as the 1920s, in the chapel at Alençon built over the former garden of the house where Thérèse was born, people were dedicating plaques to her that still testify to their trust in their 'Heavenly Nurse' ('Céleste Infirmière').

The title of Thérèse's autobiography explains why she has come to be known as the 'Little Flower', but why did she give herself this title? Thérèse wrote the story of her soul when instructed to do so by her sister and spiritual mentor, Pauline, who had become Reverend Mother of her Carmel. It was not written with publication in mind but as something approaching a memento of Thérèse's family life and of her ideas. It was to be circulated on her death only to close relatives and to a select number of Carmels. The term 'Little Flower' was not offered self-consciously as a useful form of reference or address for an anticipated wider readership or audience. It was chosen in the first place because the Martins often used the image of a flower as a kind of family shorthand. Throughout her manuscript Thérèse calls herself *the* little white flower in homage to her father's symbolic plucking of a saxifrage from the wall on 29 May 1887 (Pentecost) to acknowledge her announcement that she wanted to enter Carmel. Thérèse was brought up to see the world as many-sided, as a world of flowers and people, and so on, that were real because they were sustained by God. She understood what she experienced simply and directly but also 'metaphorically', in the tradition of the imagery of the Psalms and New Testament parables:

> I often asked myself why God has preferences, and doesn't give all souls an equal amount of grace . . . But Jesus graciously explained this mystery to me. He showed me the book of nature. Then I understood that every flower he has made is beautiful: how the rose's brilliance and the lily's whiteness don't reduce the little violet's perfume or the daisy's lovely simplicity. I saw that if all the lesser flowers wanted to be roses, nature would lose its spring-time beauty, and the fields would no longer be patterned with the hues of little flowers. It is the same in the world of souls,

which is Jesus' garden. He wanted to make great saints who may be compared to lilies and roses, but he has also created lesser ones; and these lesser ones must be content to rank as daisies and violets, flower at his feet and gladden his eyes when he looks down at them, for perfection means doing his will, being what he wants us to be . . .

I also understood that our Lord's love is shown to us as much in the simplest soul that does not resist his grace as in the most highly endowed. In fact, since the nature of love is to make yourself small, if all souls resembled the holy Doctors who have illumined the Church . . . it would seem as if God weren't stooping low enough when he came into *their* hearts. But he has created little children, who know nothing about anything and can only make themselves heard by feeble crying; and he has made the poor savages, who have only the natural law to follow; and it is to their hearts that he is willing to come down. These are the wild flowers whose simplicity charms him, and it is by his condescension to them that God shows his infinite greatness. The same sun's light that shines on the cedar-tree shines uniquely on the smallest flower. Just so, our Lord concentrates on each soul uniquely, and everything works together for the good of each soul, just as in nature the seasons are arranged to ensure that the humblest daisy will unfold its petals on the appointed day . . .

If a little flower could talk, I think it would say quite simply what God had done for it, and not hide any of his gifts. It wouldn't say, in mock humility, that it wasn't pretty and didn't smell sweet, that the sun had withered its petals or a storm bruised its stem, if it knew all that wasn't true. The flower now telling her tale is delighted to record our Lord's wholly undeserved favours. She knows that in herself she had nothing that could have drawn his attention, for it was his mercy that put anything good in her – his mercy alone.

He decided that she was to be born in holy ground fragrant with the scent of purity. He made sure that eight dazzling white

lilies sprang up there before she appeared. He loved his little
flower so much that he wanted to protect her from the poisoned
air of the world, for her petals had hardly unfolded when her
divine Master transplanted her to Mount Carmel . . .[7]

Carmel means 'an orchard' or 'garden', and the fragrant
trees, plants and flowers of the Carmel range of mountains
suggested the Garden of Eden to the Hermits of Our Lady of
Mount Carmel, the original Carmelites. In our end is our
beginning. A key description in the opening scenes of the
Bible is that of the garden lovingly designed and laid out for
humankind by God; and Thérèse, a little white flower in the
chosen enclosure of her life, reflects that love throughout the
pages that follow.

The imagery of flowers recurs like a refrain in the three
separate manuscripts that make up what we now think of as
Thérèse's 'autobiography': Manuscript A(gnes), written in
1895–6 at the instigation of her sister Pauline when Prioress;
Manuscript B (or M[arie]), written during Thérèse's last
retreat (8–13 September 1896) at the request of her eldest sister,
Sister Marie of the Sacred Heart; and the unfinished Manuscript C (or G[onzague]), requested by Mother Gonzague at
the prompting of Pauline, and begun in June 1897.

Manuscript A begins with references to the 'little white
flower', charts its nurture and flowering, and ends with its
readiness to be picked or transplanted. In Manuscript B the
petals of the flower have blossomed and are scattered and
strewn for the sake of love: 'I want to suffer and rejoice for
Love's sake, and so I shall strew my flowers.' Finally, in Manuscript C, written when Thérèse's life was ebbing away and left
as it now ends, just three months before her death, the flower
also reaches the limits of fullness and self-surrender. This
manuscript refers to dew deep in the calyx, to perfumes, and
to the 'fragrance of the ointments of the Beloved'. It moves

forward to the moment when nothing remains of all this but the luminous, perfumed traces Jesus has left behind, and Thérèse steers her way towards him by following these atoms of love radiating through eternity, inhaling their energy until she can throw herself into his arms.

Thérèse was an artist. Most worthwhile artists have drawn inspiration from the past in order to express their particular visions in a new way relevant to their own times and the occasions of their lives. To express her own special vision, Thérèse calls on the Bible, on her family, on the saints, religious authors, poets of nature and the infinite, and on her experience of nature and her immediate environment.

For Thérèse, flowers are metaphorical in the biblical sense. They are symbolic reflections of divine beauty and love, chalices of openness to the inpouring of God. They are human lives that come up, bud, bloom and have but a short time to live before they are cut down in fragile reliance on the vagaries of nature: on rain, drought, darkness and cold; and on wind and storm – all parts of a divine order. The individual flower that is Thérèse depends on the light of Jesus the Sun, but also on the earth where she is rooted and from which she springs: in other words, on her father and mother, and on her sisters and Sisters in God (often the same). This little flower is a wild flower of the fields tamed by the arrangement of the flower-bed and garden which God has designed for her nurture, so that she can rest in obscure readiness to serve and to please when she is seen or is offered as a mark of love. The holy ground in which Thérèse locates herself as a flower may be her home or Carmel, earth as a whole, and even the great expanses of the cosmos, but also the pastoral setting so often invoked in the Old and New Testaments.

At the beginning of her autobiography Thérèse speaks of God's constant loving care for her and, in the context of her flower imagery, quotes Psalm 23 (22), a central reference that brings together the principal themes of her writings:

> I am now at a time in my life when I can look back on the past, for my soul has been refined in the crucible of outward and inward trials. Like a flower after the storm, I can raise my head and see in myself the meaning of these words:
>
>> The Lord is my shepherd; I shall not want;
>> He makes me lie down in green pastures.
>> He leads me beside still waters;
>> He restores my soul.
>> He leads me in right paths
>> for his name's sake.[8]

The paths and pastures in which she walks are simultaneously biblical and those of her Norman childhood. From her infancy onwards, Thérèse had observed the details of her natural surroundings. She admired and drew inspiration from the broad views and the great pines with their branches sweeping to the ground, the rivers, and the wild flowers of the fields and seashores of France. All these impressions were imprinted on her very being and fed her natural lyrical impulse, her sense of the poetry of existence.

Poetry as literary composition was another important influence in Thérèse's early life. She loved reading. Of course she read approved prose fiction for children, and she was fond of the popular red-bound volumes of the *Bibliothèque rose* containing tales by Madame de Ségur, Canon Schmidt, and others. They were moralizing, but amenably so, since they were usually about recognizably real children in a real environment. But the verse she read and listened to at home had a more vital effect on her than the elegantly expressed strictures of Boileau's *Art poétique*, the seventeenth-century treatise on the art of poetry, which she studied under Madame Papinau, her teacher in 1886–7.

From Boileau she learned such principles as the need to maintain a noble style and to remain faithful to nature, stated in easily-memorized rhyming couplets that have re-echoed in the heads of French schoolchildren for generations.[9] The freshness and clarity of her autobiography and letters show that even in her prose composition Thérèse took to heart his insistence on good sense and his dislike of affectation. In her poems, too, she followed Boileau's canons of good formal composition as she understood them, and her plays reveal a knowledge of his rules for writing dramatic verse appropriate to theme and occasion. Nevertheless, Alphonse de Lamartine (1790–1869) and Victor Hugo (1802–1885), the stalwarts of nineteenth-century late Romantic French verse, were her main models in poetry.

In the evening Thérèse's father would often recite poems by Lamartine[10] and Hugo,[11] and images and specific words and phrases (even if not always perfectly recalled) from these poets resurface in her autobiography and other writings. She would have heard repeatedly such famous lines of Lamartine's as 'Born with the spring, dying with the roses',[12] 'You sow the ground of our harsh life with signs of hope, like flowers embroidered on a winding-sheet',[13] 'Let us gather, let us gather roses in the morning of life',[14] '. . . flowers, new-born prayers with corollas filled with honey by God himself, lily-pure, rose-chaste, seem to intercede for us in these heavenly mansions',[15] and one that Monsieur Martin used almost as a mantra: 'Time is your boat and not your home!'[16] (which Thérèse – possibly by design – misquoted as 'life is your boat . . .' and related to the 'ship that sails through the billowy water, and when it has passed no trace can be found' of Wisdom 5:10). Lamartine's sonorous verses, with their constant references to flowers as the incense of the world, to nature and solitude, to a devoutly-wished-for death, and to the soul or earth as a ship, and their injunctions to Christian souls to face suffering with love in acknowledgement of Love ('Aimons!', 'C'est lui, c'est l'amour!') echo throughout her works.

Similarly, the Hugo who left a mark on Thérèse's writing was not the dramatist and novelist, and scarcely the great cosmic visionary, but the lyrical poet who paid as much attention to 'local colour' as to meditation on the mystery of death and the ultimate triumph of good over evil. Her Hugo was the solitary who saw: '. . . a white angel passing overhead . . . I asked: "Are you life or death?"/And the angel turned black, and said: "I am love" ';[17] for whom 'For God the blessed are not those who find but those who search.'[18] In one of his best-known poems, *Oneness*, a humble daisy looks up at the sun, a great flower in the vastness of eternity, and says: 'I, too, shine in my own way!'

> Bloom of everlasting radiance bright,
> Beyond the horizon's fine-burnished rim
> The sun at close of day to earth inclined.
> And, on an old grey wall where oats encroached,
> A mere daisy in a field, simple, white,
> Opened its guileless glory to the sky.
> Over the ruined wall the little flower,
> With steady gaze at blue immensity,
> Where the great star poured forth immortal light,
> Declared: 'With my own rays I also shine.'[19]

Thérèse was indebted not only to the literary great and good of late French Romanticism but to a less renowned writer. She wrote poems that reveal the influence of the Norman peasant poet, Rose Harel, who was born in the village of Bellou in 1826 and died on 5 July 1885. Rose taught herself to read when she was thirteen and was given lessons in writing by a friend. She went to live in Vimoutiers, where she worked as a weaver, then went into service in Pont-l'Evèque and later in Lisieux. She produced two volumes of poetry: *Lark in the Cornfield* (*L'alouette aux blés*) in 1863 (2nd edition, 1864) and *Autumn Flowers* (*Fleurs d'automne*) in 1885, the latter with a preface by the Lisieux novelist Marie de Besneray. Rose's poems won her a not inconsiderable local reputation in her lifetime, especially among families such as the Martins of Lisieux. They contain many descriptions of the Norman countryside and often focus on some of Thérèse's favourite flowers, as in:

> 'The Daisy'
> You know the wild flower,
> Yes, that one, small and neat,
> Lover's bloom, enchanter's herb,
> We call the Marguerite.
> Hiding for the heart alone
> Under its corolla – look! –
> Unfolding petals, pages
> In a holy, secret book.

or:

> 'Bengal Roses'
> I know what I would do:
> Build a cottage
> Where the stream runs,
> If I were rich as you.
>
> See the primrose leave its seed,
> Hear the water softly sound,
> The rustling of the heather,
> The wind talking to a reed.

Then I would ask the muse
To teach me everything:
The perfume of the rose,
The water's bitter truth —
Secrets no words can sing.[20]

The real world of Rose's poems was much the same as the meadows through which Thérèse and her father passed on their long walks together and the river banks where they sat listening to the wind. Her flowers and country images are reflected in such statements in Thérèse's verses as 'I loved the cornfields and the plains . . . I loved to gather grassy stems, cornflowers, all the little flowers . . . and the heather.'[21] Rose's yearning for another state of being, and her far from simplistic understanding of the duality of existence and its expression in quite subtly rehandled even if stock imagery, also have their counterparts in Thérèse's compositions in prose and verse.

Thérèse's practical knowledge of the flora of the natural world, and her impressions of their literary and other metaphorical uses were unified by a now almost entirely forgotten book she received from her Benedictine abbey school in 1884 as a prize for good conduct. It was obviously chosen by someone who was well aware of Thérèse's particular combination of interests. One might even think, indeed, that this was a work written specially for her. The Abbé Aquilas Chaudé's *The Theology of Plants* (*La Théologie des plantes, ou Histoire intime du monde végétal* [1882], and subtitled 'an intimate history of the vegetal world') was a recent publication, yet one wholly untouched by Darwinian ideas or any of the biological, geological and botanical observations and research that might hint at any form of evolutionary theory. The Church at the time, as evidenced by various nineteenth-century encyclicals and a great number of pronouncements and publications at different levels of authority, rejected any notions that seemed to challenge a literal interpretation of Scripture and the strict creationism derived from it. Chaudé's book was entirely trustworthy in this respect. He was the parish priest of Vaujours (in the Seine-Marne, near Meaux) and produced a long work of lyrical prose combining his own observations and his readings of the Swedish botanist Linnaeus, Rousseau, and the many devotional works that described the universe, especially the starry sky above, as evidence of divine omnipotence and loving kindness. For Chaudé, however, the study of plants was the 'visible ladder by which human beings approach the invisible creator of the universe', and the glory of God was declared in little things, in plants and in the details of their structure and growth:

The corolla is the empress of the vegetal world and might surely be a star fallen from the heavens, a daughter of paradise astray on this earth. The stars of the firmament shining above us do not possess the scent and variety of these earthly stars. Moreover, as I stand on the shores of this ocean of shapes, colours and perfumes, the more I contemplate all these glories, the more clearly and unmistakably I recognize the brush, manner and style of the divine artist and decorator of the universe. Humans came thereafter and though they labour from morning to night their faint handiwork can scarcely enumerate these multitudinous countenances, enunciate the various nuances of these beauteous forms, or calculate the numberless companies of these wonders . . . sparkling in the grass, climbing in shrubbery, springing from bushes, dropping as if in cascades from the very tops of our forests, and bestowing their garlands on the cottages of the poor and the palaces of the rich . . . We realize that the fundamental cell of the entire plant is actively present, full and ready in the fine tissues and beneath the unrivalled colouration of the corolla, proclaiming the hand of God.[22]

For Chaudé, as for Thérèse, the harmonies and operations of this 'veritable chemical laboratory' obeyed their divine impulse, constantly transforming their essence and appearance until they reached their individual culmination, showing forth God's love to humankind. Flowers were a summary manifestation of 'all created beings, visible and invisible: soul and matter, images of God and epitomes of the universe'. His flower calendar and flower clock, but especially his detailed accounts of the development of plants from the mysterious combination of chemical elements, through the unfolding of their organs, flowering, fertilization and fruiting, to their enduring of sickness and submission to death, provided much of Thérèse's knowledge of human and extra-human biology. They also enriched her imagery of physical and spiritual development and gave it a unifying structure.

She also listened to and read, at home, at school, in her convent, and by way of the regular formal readings there, major devotional and spiritual, even mystical works that helped to form the network of images she used to tell her story.

François-René de Chateaubriand's *The Genius of Christianity* (*La Génie du Christianisme*),[23] sub-titled 'the Poetic and Moral Beauties of the Christian Religion' (1802), was certainly among the Martins' Catholic books. It was available throughout the nineteenth century in countless popular and gift editions for adults and older children. It stressed not only the rational appeal of dogmatic Christianity and its importance as a moral and liberating, lyrical and human force, but the ways in which the great artistic and literary creations of Christianity shaped the human understanding of and empathy with the natural world.

Thérèse was also familiar with some of the great works of Christian spirituality and mysticism. *The Imitation of Christ* by Thomas à Kempis was one of her favourite books at home.

The author and Thérèse are in complete agreement that one should never worry, as she puts it, about being unable to 'reason, discuss, argue and explain'. She returned to the 'pure flour' of the *Imitation* frequently, carried it about with her tucked into her pocket or muff, learned almost the entire book by heart (though Céline said she knew every line), and could recite any chapter when her aunt opened the book at random. Its commonsense recommendations and something of its style ('There are no frills about the *Imitation*. It has the frill-lessness of Euclid and the Athanasian Creed.'[24]) became her own:

Some people, for want of prudence, have brought about their own downfall through the grace of devotion. They wanted to do more than they were able, taking no account of their own little-ness . . . It is a great thing to be among the least in heaven, where all are great; because all there shall be called, and shall really be, the children of God.

Not only à Kempis' advice on cultivating fruitful simplicity and humility but something akin to his mystical fervour became a major element in Thérèse's own writing:

Anyone in love treads on air and runs for very joy . . . Let my love know no bounds; let me learn to taste with the lips of my inmost being how sweet it is to love, to melt in love's fire, to float on the waves of love! . . . Pour down your grace from above; soak my heart with the rain of heaven; bring me streams of devotion to water the face of this earth, to make it bear good and perfect fruit.[25]

In Carmel, the extracts from the mystical treatises of Sts John of the Cross and Teresa of Avila that she read and heard enhanced this particular mode of expression, which became

part of her devotional awareness along with more circum-
stantial descriptions and plain statements. She was particularly
moved by the writings of St John of the Cross, and what she
understood as his message about divine wisdom, her Beloved,
instructing the soul and speaking to her 'in silence, in darkness'. He remained a lifelong influence: 'I have received much
spiritual light through the works of St John of the Cross, and
at the age of seventeen and eighteen they were my only
food.'[26] Her writing often reflects and she specifically refers to
and quotes St John's imagery of the vineyard in flower as the
nursery of the works and virtues that, even if humanly perfect,
are spiritually dry unless brought to blossom by God's grace
and love; and his portrayal of the soul offering her fragrance
and sweetness to her Beloved as a nosegay of roses, or perfect
virtues combined and ordered into one firm perfection of the
soul, and thus driving away the 'foxes', those discordant yet
subtly malicious thoughts, images, and terrors of the psyche
that threaten spiritual flowers:

O woods and thickets planted by the hand of the Beloved!
O meadow of verdure, enamelled with flowers,
Say if he has passed by you.
Scattering a thousand graces, he passed through these
groves in haste,
And, looking upon them as he went, left them, by his
glance alone, clothed with beauty . . .
Drive away the foxes, for our vineyard is now in flower,
While we make a bunch of roses, and let none appear upon the hill.
Stay you, dead north wind. Come, south wind, that awakens love;
Breathe through my garden and let your odours flow, and the Beloved
shall pasture among the flowers.[27]

In addition to these more mystical influences, the continuing Jansenist strain in French Catholicism, though officially

disavowed, should not be underestimated when defining Thérèse's spiritual heritage. Nevertheless, a particular tradition of French eighteenth-century spirituality, that of Francis (François) de Sales, Jeanne de Chantal, de Bérulle, de Condren, Mme Acarie, Jean-Jacques Olier, John (Jean) Eudes, Louis Lallemant, Joseph Surin, and Mary of the Incarnation (Marie de l'Incarnation), exerted a greater influence through her mentors, in particular her two oldest sisters, and some of her reading. There was something like a minor revival of this French school of mysticism around the time of Thérèse's birth.

Above all, St Francis de Sales and the Visitandine inheritance helped to form those aspects of Thérèse's religious attitudes that suited his combination of humility, serenity and simplicity. The guidance of her sister Pauline, who had been educated at a Visitation convent, was an important influence here. Of course, there was another reason for Thérèse to favour de Sales. After Thérèse's birth it seemed that she was in danger of death, so her aunt vowed to St Francis de Sales that if the little girl survived she would be named after him. Accordingly, her full name was Marie-Françoise Thérèse Martin and Francis de Sales became one of her spiritual protectors. Thérèse was careful to enter the initials 'FMT' (Marie-Françoise Thérèse) in the right-hand section of the coat-of-arms she designed and which appears at the end of Manuscript A. During the preliminary investigation into the cause for Thérèse's beatification, her sister Léonie, a nun of the Visitation Order, remarked:

> In all our convents Sister Thérèse is greatly revered; that is not surprising, since the spirit of her piety is entirely ours and that of our founder, St Francis de Sales . . . My spirituality is that of my Thérèse, and therefore that of our saintly Founder. His teaching and hers are just the same. She is the very soul whom our great Founder was thinking of.[28]

Léonie's enthusiasm was understandable if a little overplayed, for St Francis' manual was addressed to women 'in the world' whose spiritual lives he was directing. He wanted to show them how to think and behave in ways that would please God yet not demand neglect of their secular responsibilities. They were women of a station somewhat different to that of Thérèse, and they appreciated their director's wit and learning.

Much of the rich imagery of de Sales' *An Introduction to the Devout Life* is drawn from everyday life, the natural world and science (though the details come from antiquated sources such as the ancient Roman encyclopaedia of natural science by the Elder Pliny). Even if the applications are down-to-earth, the references are as often literary as proverbial, and even pleasingly academic, as de Sales cites the classics of antiquity or the Fathers of the Church. His flower images are among the best-known passages in the book, and help to point the differences between the traditional use of garden imagery in spiritual works and Thérèse's own method. De Sales' metaphors are disparate, and chosen according to the situation dealt with, whereas Thérèse's similes are parts of a coherent metaphorical whole, the story of the Little Flower in which she is also merely a little flower. Nevertheless, she will have known the famous opening and an associated passage, understood their relevance to her own reading and practice, and included them in the complex of thought and feeling she drew on when writing:

> Glycera, the flower-seller, was so skilled at arranging flowers that she could take one sort of flowers and make a great number of different bouquets from them. In fact, when the painter Pausias tried to draw Glycera's various bouquets, he found the task impossible. He just couldn't apply his skill in painting to the profusion of bouquets she had made up. In the same way, the

Holy Spirit has a vast number of ways of inspiring and arranging advice on how to lead a devout life, when he presents it through the words and writings of his helpers. The doctrine, to be sure, is always the same, but the writings in which it appears are very different because of the variety of ways used to put them together.[29]

Why not try gathering a little nosegay of devotion . . . People who have been walking in a beautiful garden are reluctant to leave without taking away four or five flowers in order to breathe in their fragrance as they carry them about for the rest of the day. Similarly, after meditating on some mystery, we should pick out one or two or three points that we found most engaging and could help us to improve ourselves. We should recall them throughout the day, and inhale their spiritual fragrance.[30]

Just as Thérèse's use of metaphor was influenced by a poet less illustrious than Lamartine and Hugo, so her vision was affected by a writer of religiously intended prose on a much lower level of literary competence and of breadth and nobility of mind than those of Thomas à Kempis and Francis de Sales. The greatest artists, writers and thinkers have sometimes found inspiration in cranky and even tawdry models which, by one of the inexplicable miracles of the creative life, prompt thoughts and works that far surpass them.

In May–June 1887, when she was fourteen, Thérèse happened on and read with increasing excitement a book by the French priest and preacher Charles Arminjon (1824–1885), which her father had borrowed from the nuns of the Lisieux Carmel. *The End of this World and the Mysteries of the World to Come (Fin du monde présent et mystères de la vie future*, 1881) contained a mass of inconsistencies, anti-Semitic rant, crude religiosity, and ill-informed astro-scientific projections. It also offered an eschatological vision of a redeemed natural world that confirmed and revitalized Thérèse's understanding of a natural and human environment to which she saw herself returning after death to carry out her commission of love. Arminjon's view of reality was much more attractive than the traditional contempt for the actual world recommended by à Kempis and others. Her 'reading of this book became one of the greatest graces in my life ... All the great truths of religion, the secrets of eternity, gave me a joy which was no longer of this earth'.

> This world is an immense laboratory in which nature as a whole is fermenting and labouring . . . All the stars and all the suns have been regenerated by the blood of God and have shared in the grace of the Redemption . . . Our earth is the centre of the supernatural world because its material substance is undergoing a continuous process of transubstantiation as the Body of God is consumed in the Eucharist . . . Do not think that just because the world will have ceased to turn on its axis and to follow its familiar course, like a slave in a tread-mill, that in the new earth the air will have lost its freshness, the fields will no longer be green, the trees will have lost their blossom, and water will no longer spring from fountains. The new world to come is a living thing . . . This world is in travail, sowing the future harvest in tears and suffering, but sooner or later the sun of that other world whose dawn we can see with the eyes of faith will rise on this world of ours . . . Jesus wanted to trace out two contrary ways of reaching heaven: one, for himself, that was rough and mortifying; and another, for his followers, that was pleasant, and planted with roses and joyous occasions.[31]

This idea of the remaking of the natural world and of humankind reinforced Thérèse's developing notion of what it meant to be a saint. This world and its inhabitants were made and destined to realize their full potential in heaven. That would not mean dehumanized shades languishing in a quite distinct universe, but the fulfilment of intensities of nature and of humanity that could be glimpsed now. Death, even martyrdom, would not be an entitlement to everlasting repose. It would mean increasingly heightened activity on behalf of this world, and even in this world. That was how Thérèse came to understand the words inscribed on the wall of Carmel as she climbed the twenty-three stairs that led to her cell, and engaged in actual effort and symbolic ascesis: 'A little labour today, eternal rest tomorrow . . .'. When she knew she was close to death she told those around her: 'Don't think when I'm gone that I shall be content to look down from the height of heaven. Certainly not! I shall come down from there!'[32]

Everyone was destined to be a saint. Everyone must be a saint. The ideal was attainable by growing and flowering as one was destined to grow and flower. Sainthood was recognizable not only in the imagery and injunctions of devout manuals and sacred texts but in the vitality of one's own aspirations and of those like oneself. It was visible in their activity now, the first phase of a never-ending apostolate.

In 1896 Thérèse read the biography of her ideal saint. He was the young missionary and 'little martyr', Théophane Vénard (1829–1861), who was beheaded at Tonkin, in Indo-China. The book 'interested me and touched me more than I could express'. He was very much like her, she thought. He had a similar conception of mission and destiny, deep affection for his close family circle, and the same lively temperament. He was a soul-mate in a very special sense. His example reinforced her desire to join the Carmelites in either Saigon or Hanoi. She was especially taken by the published selection of Théophane's letters, and copied extracts from them:

Truly the Lord chooses little people to put the great of this world to confusion . . . When my head is severed by the executioner's axe, Immaculate Mother, receive your little servant like a ripe grape fallen from the knife, like a full-blown rose plucked in your honour . . . I have reached the point each of us has desired for so long! Martyrdom! . . . The light movement of a blade will separate my head from my body like a spring flower which the owner of the garden gathers for his delight. We are all flowers planted on this earth and God gathers us up in his own good time, some earlier, others later. The crimson rose has its own uniqueness, as does the virginal lily and the humble violet. Let us all try to please our supreme Lord and Master by realizing the particular scent and lustre that we have been given.[33]

In May–June 1897, a few months before her death, Thérèse copied several key phrases from Théophane's letters onto the back of an engraving of the Child Jesus gathering roses in his garden that she had enhanced with quotations for her sisters. She intensely disliked images of death as the traditional grim reaper or a skeleton in a plumed hat, and asked Pauline to remove one from the copy of La Fontaine's *Fables* she had borrowed from her sister. 'Not "Death" but God who loves us will come looking for me,' she said. 'Death isn't the phantom or vile spectre shown in all those pictures.' In the words of Théophane Vénard, which she adapted and inscribed on her 'memorial card': 'I am a spring flower gathered by the owner of the garden for his delight. We are all flowers planted on this earth and God gathers us up in his own good time, some earlier, others later. I am an ephemeral little creature, and I shall be the first to go.'[34] Thérèse's mature image of human purpose and destiny, of coming into existence, growing in sanctity, and realizing it fully, was one of flowering as a smile of God in a garden of love.

❧ 1 ❧

The Virtues of Flowers

Only a soul that has been made pure will understand the fragrance of the rose.

Paul Claudel

The roses had the look of flowers that are looked at.

T. S. Eliot

I was always fond of flowers.

Thérèse of Lisieux

Thérèse believed that we need images to understand spiritual matters.[1] When she wrote or spoke of flowers she used a universal symbol that can be appreciated by everyone, rich or poor, religious or non-religious. Of course she clearly loved real flowers and, like most of us, was delighted by their colours and scents and the childhood memories they evoked.

Florigraphy is a science that requires little study. The meanings associated with some flowers now seem almost automatic. There are few nations that do not recognize the rose as an emblem of love and the daisy as standing for innocence. Nevertheless, in our age of virtual reality, when so many people are cut off from the rhythms and cycles of the natural world, it is difficult to empathize with people living in the nineteenth century, when the symbolic value of flowers was much more significant than nowadays. Flowers and bouquets were given, deposited or thrown on all but a few occasions, whether joyous or sad, and each variety or colour of flower had a particular meaning.

A flower seems to contain all the elements of nature: ether, air, water, fire and earth. It has form, colour, texture, fragrance and the mysterious quality of a living thing in which we sense the vibrations of something abstract, pure and perfect, and otherwise indefinable.

Thérèse's family used the language of flowers as a kind of shorthand, and in her daily study of the Bible, religious writers and holy pictures, she absorbed the references to nature and flowers as emblems of spiritual truths. Her novice mistress, Marie of the Angels and the Sacred Heart, was one of the first people to remark on Thérèse's use of flower imagery. She said that the role Thérèse attributed to flowers was an aspect of her piety that particularly impressed her, because she had never heard it spoken of in Carmel or mentioned in the lives of the saints:

> For her, every flower spoke a language of its own, in which it revealed God's infinite love and perfections to her. She also used them to tell God of her own love and other sentiments. Late on a summer's evening, in the time of silence, and often on a feast day at recreation, she would strew flowers round the base of the Calvary in the cloister garth.[2]

Thérèse saw flowers as symbols of 'souls in Jesus' garden'[3] and herself as an insignificant little white flower growing there. Her message is one of 'littleness', of her 'little way'. This does not mean arranging one's life as a series of minor sacrifices but accepting oneself and living as God intended one to be, whether in obscurity or in an exalted position. For Thérèse, Carmel was an enclosed garden where she could remain hidden and inconspicuous. She saw death not as a grim reaper but as Jesus taking up his harvest of flowers, and knew that she would be 'gathered in the springtime of her life'.[4]

Roses

Although Thérèse thought of herself essentially as a 'little white flower', she used other floral images, including the emblematic rose, to express her thoughts and feelings. Since her death, Thérèse has always been associated with roses, not only because she promised to 'make it rain with roses after my death',[5] and only fifteen days before she died called herself a 'springtime rose' (*rose printanière*) in connection with the rose whose petals she arranged round a crucifix,[6] but because roses signify love. She referred to roses at other points in *The Story of a Soul* and in conversations published later, but the link was reinforced initially by the dissemination of cards, illustrations, statuettes and medals based mainly on Céline's original 1912 charcoal portrait, and on her 1925 coloured version of the same image, of Thérèse holding roses in the traditional manner of virgins and other saints in paintings, statues and popular 'holy pictures'.[7]

Céline's impulse to embellish her photographs of Thérèse was matched by the overwhelming public response to her sister as a beautiful and fragrant rose. The vision of Thérèse as a rose and saint of roses tended to overshadow her image as a simple 'little white flower', and encouraged sentimental distortions as often as profound spiritual analogies. Thérèse's real message of 'littleness', love and abandonment to God's will, of simplicity, childlikeness, and the beauty and value of all nature, whether a drop of dew, a wild or a common garden flower, or a magnificent perfumed rose, was obscured.

Over the years the association with roses became so strong that in 1997, when the Pope made Thérèse a Doctor of the

Church, Lisieux's Socialist Council (with a rose as its symbol) and Mayor (Yvette Roudy, formerly a Minister for Women's Rights) decided to give the town an appropriate face-lift by planting 50,000 roses, and a local horticulturalist created a special 'rosier Sainte-Thérèse' for the occasion.[8]

Naturally the rise and establishment of the association of roses with Thérèse that led to such practices depended on much more than either her promise to let fall a beneficial shower of petals, or imitations of Céline's image of her as a rose-bearer. The connection was nurtured by Thérèse's own various, and variously significant, references to roses, other flowers and plants, gardens and growth, at first in *The Story of a Soul*, and later in her poems, plays, letters, and reported conversations, as these gradually became available to an ever-larger public, at first in selections and then in full editions. Some of these echoes and associations were evident and intended, others unconscious, and yet others added by readers later. For example, the sixth of a series of poems that Thérèse wrote (instead of a playlet) for her Sisters, to be recited during the Pious Recreation of Christmas 1895, directly mentions and contrasts yet also reconciles the lily and the rose:

> Sweet-scented spirit of delight,
> For Jesus, Mary, blossom white,
> Hear your Beloved softly speak
> This secret to your soul so meek:
> 'I love the lily's guiltless glow,
> But also the rose, its sorrow,
> Its richly-coloured tears that smart,
> Yet wash all hatred from the heart.
> Then, infinite joy, I gather
> All these flowers for my Father.'[9]

Here the red rose stands not only, as in common tradition, for love but for penitence, a somewhat more unusual, if traditional, association. The description of the lily's white innocence and simplicity serves to emphasize the rich colour and high price of the rose, restored to harmony by its own sorrow and potential for love, and by the lily's humility and service, but only within God's all-encompassing forgiveness. As so often in Thérèse's writings, a lyrical and symbolic account of a moral truth or situation and of its transcendental implications is linked to her own experience or to that of her community. Here there is an implicit reference to Hyacinthe Loyson, a former Carmelite priest who had left not only the Order but the Church in order to be married. Thérèse prayed constantly for him and called him 'our brother', or a 'lost sheep', whereas for the Catholic papers he was a 'renegade priest'.[10]

As in this instance, though to varying degrees, the association of roses with Thérèse relied not merely on her own statements and analogies, or on a specific person or event, named or implied, but on a multitude of secular, that is, literary and popular, and religious implications of rose and flower imagery extending back not merely into Christian usage but into antiquity, and maintained in social customs, regional legends, verse, devotional texts and practices, hymns, and various liturgies and rites of the Church.

The Rose in Myth and Folklore

The rose is an ancient plant: 'Oh! no one knows / Through what wild centuries / Roves back the Rose!'[11] It evolved to withstand hostile environments from the Siberian snows to the rays of an Egyptian sun. In classical antiquity roses were as popular and carried as many metaphorical echoes as in the Christian centuries. In Roman poetry the brief lifespan of the rose and the promise of rose gardens blasted by the south wind of the morning stood for the brevity of human existence and the fragility of its sweetness. In ancient Greece mourners wore roses and strewed them on graves (a practice initially prohibited though eventually accepted by the Christian Church), and Sophocles' tomb is said to have been laden with them. May was a favoured month for offering roses to the spirits of the dead. In Rome the annual feast of roses, when tombs were adorned with garlands, was known as *rosales escae*, and the ceremony itself as *rosalia*. The wills of wealthy Romans often asked for roses to be planted on their resting-places, or left funds for rose gardens to provide fresh tributes for tombs on the anniversaries of their deaths. The rose festivals of later years recalled those honouring the goddess Flora in the ancient world. The floral games of Toulouse, in France, were revived when the poet Clemence Isaure (d. 1540) left a fortune to provide poetry prizes at flower festivals in early May that began with the strewing of roses over Clemence's tomb. These ancient traditions, as well as his own wish to die while roses were in bloom, came into play when Victor Hugo's coffin was heaped with roses in May 1885.

Throughout Europe folktales and ballads bear witness to oral traditions of roses growing from graves to signify virginity or eternal love, but also to powerful taboos associated with their wanton plucking by the cold of heart or by any person other than the dead girl's sweetheart.

In folklore the purity of the rose was said to ward off evil spirits, for those possessed by them ran shrieking from the scent of roses; if asked to pluck roses, clandestine sorcerers and vampires were forced to reveal their perfidy; and a rose bush was a sure means of restoring a werewolf to human form. Rose water, by derivation, was held to possess an anti-demonic virtue, and vessels of it were used at appropriate points in ceremonies. Before the future poet Ronsard was baptized his nurse dropped him on a heap of flowers while another woman poured rose water over him.

In various parts of Europe a virtuous girl (known in France as a *rosière*) was crowned with white roses or carried a wreath of them before the coffin of a virgin. The garland would hang over the dead girl's pew in church until the flowers faded, a custom reflected in the Carmelite practice of placing a wreath of roses on the head of a dead nun. When one of the Sisters with influenza whom Thérèse was nursing died, she would put such a wreath on the nun's head, as the Rule required.[12]

Roses and Love, Earthly and Divine

In most cultures flowers, especially roses, stand for love. This was an essential aspect of flower symbolism for Thérèse, too, who knew her vocation was 'to be love in the heart of the Church' reaching out to embrace the whole world.[13] Her use of the rose to represent love stood in a long tradition of Christian and pre-Christian culture in which it came to signify the interconnected states of mind and body, the movements of heart and soul, the fount of life and mystical centre of the universe evoked by the lotus in Asia, but also by the cosmic rose Triparasundari in India, which symbolizes the beauty of the divine Mother. Depth psychologists such as Jung have remarked on the closeness in form of lotus and rose to the wheel as a mandala, or religious symbol of individual longing for fullness and for unity of different aspects turning on the infinite centre of all being, as in the rose windows of cathedrals.

Rose symbolism is found in many of the great literary works of the ages of faith, in the thirteenth-century allegory of courtly love known as the *Roman de la Rose*, for instance, but above all in Dante's *Divine Comedy*. There the vision of a spiritual order as the goal of every life focuses on the vast symbolic rose of dazzling whiteness and ultimate freedom that Beatrice shows her faithful lover as he approaches the last circle of Paradise, having passed through the hells of inward and outward suffering until purified by gradual self-awareness and by love. The petals are the souls of the blessed and between them angels fly in and out of the rose. Its golden centre promises the final vision of the heavenly Love that moves the sun and other stars:

> There is in heaven a light, whose goodly shine
> Makes the Creator visible to all
> Created, that in seeing him alone
> Have peace; and in a circle spreads so far,
> That the circumference were too loose a zone
> To girdle in the sun. All is one beam . . .
> Into the yellow of the rose
> Perennial, which, in bright expansiveness,
> Lays forth its gradual blooming, redolent
> Of praises to the never-wintering sun . . .
> Beatrice led me . . .[14]

Roses in Christian Iconography

In antiquity, and for the Renaissance, which revived the tradition, roses, fragrant and beautiful like the goddess of love, were the sacred flowers of Venus (Aphrodite), and originally white. Red roses, with a sexual and erotic significance drawn on by writers and artists in almost every culture to which they were known, were said to have originated when Venus trod on a thorn while hurrying to the aid of the dying Adonis, for her blood fell from the wound of love in her tender flesh and turned the white petals red. The Christian counterpart to this was the belief that Jesus was crowned with interlaced rose briars, and that the drops of blood from his forehead became the first red roses as these testimonies to his love touched the ground, or that red-petalled roses grew later from the soil on which those drops had fallen. Another tradition said that all roses were formerly red but the tears wept by Mary Magdalen during the passion soaked out the colour of one bush and produced the first white roses.

In general, among the equivalences of Christian icon-ography the red rose is the chalice holding Christ's blood, or the wound in his side, and, by derivation, stands for the blood of the martyrs. For the baroque poet Angelus Silesius each human soul is a rose because imprinted with the image of Christ's own soul of love to the point of suffering and death, yet beautiful with the promise of rebirth. St Ambrose says that the red roses of chastity grow in the garden of dedicated virginity.

To mark Thérèse's canonization, a golden rose, symbol-izing spiritual strength and knowledge, resurrection and immortality, was placed in the saint's right hand by Cardinal Vico, Pius XI's legate, on 30 September 1925. It recalled not only Dante's rose of the Empyrean but the rose or spray of roses in wrought gold set with sapphires blessed by popes on the Sunday of the Rose (*dominica rosae*), or Laetare Sunday, the fourth Sunday in Lent, and given to deserving princesses (or, later, communities). It can still be seen in her shrine at Lisieux.[15]

Saints and Roses

Thérèse's own rose and flower imagery, like that of represen-tations of her, was particularly indebted to writings of and on the saints, and to statues and other popular images of them in devotional books and in 'holy pictures', that is, prayer-book and missal cards.

Our Lady

St Ambrose refers to Mary as the 'rose of modesty' (*rosa pudoris*) and repeats an ancient legend according to which roses grew without thorns until the Fall of humankind through original sin. In countless devotions, homilies and paintings from the late Middle Ages onwards, Mary is the Mystical Rose (*Rosa mystica*) and the Rose without Thorns, because neither conceived with original sin nor sinning.

An early legend said that wherever Mary and Joseph stopped to rest during the flight into Egypt a rose, thereafter known as Mary's Rose (or the Rose of Jericho, said to revive after being dried), broke through the earth; another that when her tomb was opened, only roses and lilies were found there. She is often portrayed as St Mary of the Rose (*Santa Maria della Rosa*), when either she or the infant Jesus in her arms holds a white rose to indicate purity. She also appears as the Virgin of the Rose Garden within a paradise apart, of fragrant herbs and verdant, flower-starred lawns, combining elements taken from the Garden of Eden in Genesis and the secluded love-garden of the Song of Songs. The garden is set within a rose bower or bordered by a hedge or fence of interlaced, often red and white, roses, symbolizing blood and milk, and thus her nature, her virginity, love, compassion, humility and suffering through the passion of her Son, but also her efficacy. Sometimes yellow (that is, golden) roses are added to signify Mary's glory; or attendant angels strew rose petals on the Infant.

Our Lady's rose garden as a *hortus conclusus*, or enclosed holy garden, was particularly significant for Thérèse as a nun within Carmel, itself a sacred garden, and containing its own actual garden, one divinely symbolic enclosure within another. Its trees and plants were not wild like those in the uncontrolled natural landscape outside, but, like the Sisters who walked there, members of a family carefully chosen and cultivated, dressed to a seemly order yet open to the limitless blue above and free to receive the direct benefits of heavenly light and nurture.

Thérèse had a special devotion to Our Lady. Mary's smile healed her mysterious illness[16] on 13 May 1883, when she turned towards a statue of Our Lady.[17] It now seemed 'more beautiful than anything I had ever seen', to radiate perfect goodness and tenderness, and to smile irresistibly. She recovered from her psychosomatic sickness, although her scruples disappeared only in November 1887 when she was on her way to Rome and visited Our Lady of Victories Church in Paris.

Thérèse's first prayer that we know of was addressed to Mary, whom she asked to free her 'little Thérèse' from her constant worrying. On 8 September 1897, shortly before her death, she asked to see the image of Our Lady of Victories to which she had attached the little white flower that her father had given her when she said she wanted to enter Carmel. It was the same figure before which she had knelt to pray for guidance when writing *Story of a Soul*. She managed to write her last prayer, also to Our Lady (and modelled on one of Augustine's that she would have heard in the refectory), on its back: 'O Mary, if I were Queen of Heaven and you were Thérèse, I would want to be Thérèse so that you could be Queen of Heaven.' One day Thérèse told Céline that before she died she must write a hymn she had long dreamed of composing: a song in honour of Mary that expressed everything that she felt about Our Lady. She had never warmed to sermons about Mary that said she could not be imitated and that her glory eclipsed that of all the saints. Thérèse protested that a mother would not wish to outdo but to increase her children's glory, and said that although Mary was the Queen of Heaven and Earth, she was more Mother than Queen. She was sure that Mary's 'real life was very simple'.[18] In May 1897, the month of Mary, Thérèse summoned up all her strength to write her last poem, also to Our Lady.[19]

St Benedict (*c.* 480–547; feast, 11 July)

Roses were associated with St Benedict in the nineteenth century because those still growing at Subiaco, where he had been a hermit, were said to be descended from the original briar beds he was reputed to have planted and used to overcome temptation by rolling in them and thus mortifying his body.

St Cecilia (third century?; feast, 22 November)

The patron saint of music and musicians (because she 'sang in her heart' at her wedding) was said to have been a patrician betrothed by her father to Valerian, also a patrician but a pagan. She refused to marry Valerian because he was not a Christian, told him of her vow of chastity, and said she was guarded by an angel whom he, too, would see if he accepted baptism. Valerian promised to respect her vow. After his baptism, the angel crowned him and Cecilia with heavenly roses at a time when the natural flowers were out of season. Valerian and Cecilia were martyred for their faith. Cecilia is shown not only with a musical instrument but wearing a crown of roses. When in Italy, Thérèse (accompanied by Céline) visited Cecilia's tomb in the catacombs. She said that until she saw the actual scene of Cecilia's martyrdom she had not felt any special devotion for her, but now knew the real reason why she had been proclaimed the patron of music. It was not because of her beautiful voice, or her talent as a musician, but because of the 'sweet song she sang in her heart to her Divine Spouse':

> I felt more than devotion to her, I felt real love as for a friend. She became my chosen patroness as well as the keeper of my most intimate thoughts, for what appealed to me above all else was her

perfect abandonment to God and her unbounded confidence in him. . . . Her life was one of melodious song in the midst of terrible trials.[20]

She and Céline stretched themselves out on the site of Cecilia's tomb and took earth from it. Thérèse designed a coat-of-arms with a harp to symbolize herself singing songs of praise to Jesus.

The imagery of flowers is central to Thérèse's poem to Cecilia (28 April 1894), her first long poem, consisting originally of 120 stanzas in the manner of Lamartine, from which these verses on Cecilia's faith overcoming her suitor's ardency are taken:

> Glorious Saint of God, in ecstasy I see
> The path of shining light your footsteps left below;
> And still I think I hear your heavenly melody;
> Of your celestial chant here too the sounds we know.
> Now, of my exiled soul, accept the fervent prayer;
> Upon your virginal heart let my young heart find rest!
> Almost unequalled here were you, O lily fair,
> Immaculately pure, and how divinely blest.
>
> Most chaste white dove of Rome, through all your life on earth
> No other spouse than Christ your heart desired to find.
> He chose your precious spirit from your hour of birth,
> And made it rich in grace and virtues all combined.
> And yet a mortal came, on fire with youth and pride;
> He saw how sweet you were, O white celestial flower!
> And then, to gain your love, to win you for his bride,
> He strove with all his strength, from that momentous hour.
>   . . .
>
> In his baptismal robe, the type of innocence,
> Valerian at last the angel's face beheld;

In awe he gazed upon that grave magnificence;
That radiant, crown-decked brow his old ambitions quelled.
Fresh roses in his hands did that grand spirit bear,
Pure lilies, dazzling white, to his strong heart he pressed.
In gardens of high heaven had bloomed those blossoms rare,
Beneath the rays of love from their Creator blest.

'O Spouses dear to Heaven, the martyrs' royal rose
Shall crown your brows,' exclaimed the angel from on high.
'No voice on earth can sing, no mortal tongue disclose,
Its value beyond price, that lasts eternally.'[21]

Thérèse dedicated the poem to Céline for her twenty-first birthday. Céline was still living at home with their sick father. She had privately vowed herself to God, but was surrounded by friends who were, or were engaged to be, married. Thérèse understood her difficulties and, hoping that she could persuade Céline that she did have a religious vocation, sent her the poem and a letter to show how Cecilia's steadfastness should guide her sister's choice.

St Domitia

Domitia was reputed to have been a child martyr under the Roman persecutions and was much venerated by the Benedictine Convent of Lisieux, which received her relics in 1879. The celebration of her feast in 1881 was to be the last, for the authenticity of the relics was called in question; they were replaced by a relic of St Amata. A photograph of Domitia's shrine shows an honour ribbon of Léonie's of 1880–81. As a child, Thérèse was said to have served as the model when clothing was made for Domitia's wax effigy. On the saint's feast-day Thérèse's aunt put a pink sash (*une sinture rose*) on her and Thérèse threw rose petals at Domitia's statue.[22]

St Dorothy (Dorothea) (d. *c.*303; feast, 6 February)

Dorothy was a virgin martyr of Caesarea in Asia Minor who would not reject her Christian faith. The Roman governor sentenced her to death, and Theophilus, a scribe, was said to have mocked her on the way to execution. He asked her to send him roses and apples from Christ's heavenly gardens. After her death a child brought Theophilus a basket of roses and apples and he became a Christian; he was executed later. Although Gerard Manley Hopkins in his two poems for a picture of Dorothy portrays her with lilies, larkspur, mallow and a quince, Dorothy is usually shown holding roses, a basket of them or of roses and apples, is crowned with roses, or dies with angels bearing rose garlands flying to and fro above her. Céline's 1925 painting of Thérèse showed her in a similar stance, holding the cross and a bunch of roses.

St Elizabeth of Hungary (b. Bratislava 1207; d. Marburg 1231; feast, 17 November)

Elizabeth, founder of a hospice and carer for the poor, was the daughter of Andrew II of Hungary and patron of the Emperor Charlemagne. She practised great personal austerity in spite of ill health and repeated setbacks. She is generally shown with her apron or lap full of roses because, when her husband was hunting, she secretly took a basket of food to relieve the starving poor. He returned suddenly, demanded to see the basket, and, even though roses were out of season, found it full of choice specimens, both red and white, and divinely perfumed. Elizabeth, like Thérèse, was twenty-four when she died.

St Francis of Assisi (*c.*1182–1226; feast, 4 October)

The saint of holy poverty, compassion and 'littleness'. His total dedication to God in spite of suffering 'filled him with the sweetest fragrance' and made him 'like a rose above the rivers of flowing waters' (*quasi rosa super rivos aquarum*), that is, a flawless ideal above reflected in the flowing centuries below. He too was an 'eternal rose tree without thorns', a figure of aspiration to perfect love who told his friar-gardener he should always use some part of the garden not for 'useful' plants but to produce 'flowers for the friars, for the love of Him who is called the "flower of the field" and the "lily of the valley" ', and should set aside part of it for all sweet-smelling plants and those 'which bring forth fair flowers, that in their time they might call them that looked on these herbs and flowers to the praise of God'.[23]

Francis was a model for Thérèse in a number of ways. She said that she admired his refusal of ordination. His humility encouraged her to repress her profound longing to be a priest and channel it, in spite of her 'littleness', into what amounted to a Franciscan programme of wandering missionary endeavour with an extraordinary metaphysical élan, so that her spiritual activity would range 'back to the creation of the world and forward to the consummation of the ages'.[24] She followed his recommendation of 'joy amid life's trials and warfare',[25] using even 'our sisters, illnesses' for the greater love of God. She was inspired by his respect for women in the Church and his cult of the Child Jesus at a time notable for its anti-feminism and indifference to children, but especially by his discernment of God's presence in all, even inanimate, creatures: 'Be praised, my Lord, for our Sister Mother Earth, / who sustains and nourishes us, / and produces so many fruits, flowers of such diverse colours, and plants.'[26] When she was dying she asked to be read to from the Lives of the Saints and said that because of his humility the Life of St Francis would not tire her.[27]

St Francis de Sales (1567–1622; feast, 24 January)

Bishop and Doctor of the Church. Known to Thérèse through his spiritual treatise, *Introduction to the Devout Life*. It was followed by her father, as she records, and she copied from retreat-notes and cited pithy sayings from de Sales, such as: 'When the fire of love is in a heart all the furniture in it flies out of the windows.'[28] De Sales' insistence on a 'mild, peaceful, constant attention to the feelings of the heart', on gentle and soft self-examination (*tout bellement et doucement*), and on serenity and simplicity rather than the strenuous emotional effort and mixed fear and love of the Jesuit tradition accorded with Thérèse's practice. His presentation of his advice as a series of originally composed nosegays containing flowers of devotion from tradition, and his recommendation that those learning the ways of the devout life should do the same,[29] were major influences on her own notion of flowers and gardens as divine metaphors. St Basil the Great's emphasis on asceticism, poverty and the religious life in community as an ideal society would have been known to Thérèse, and De Sales' manual was also a channel for Basil's use of the rose metaphor with regard to tribulation:

> The great St Basil said that the rose among the thorns addresses this remonstrance to men: 'That which is most agreeable in this world, O mortals, is mingled with sadness; nothing therein is pure; regret is always joined to gladness, widowhood to marriage, care to fruitfulness, ignominy to glory, expense to honours, disgust to delights, and sickness to health. The rose indeed is a beautiful flower, but it gives me great sadness, for it reminds me of my sin, for which the earth has been condemned to bring forth thorns.'[30]

St Rosalia of Palermo (d. *c.*1166; feast, 4 September)

Rosalia, born into a noble family and the daughter of the 'lord of the roses' (*Rosarum domini filia*, that is, of the Lord of Rosae), was a Sicilian hermit vowed to chastity who appeared to victims of the plague after her death. She died alone in her cave where her uncorrupted body was found later, crowned with roses. She is shown with a crucifix and a crown of roses placed on her head by angels.

St Rose of Lima (b. Lima, Peru, 1586; d. 1617; feast, 23 August)

Rose, known as the Flower of the New World, and the patron of South America, was '*como una rosa*' (as beautiful as a rose) and mortified herself most painfully in order to reduce her worldly attractiveness and escape the marriage her parents were intent on forcing her to enter rather than the cloister. She wore a silver circlet studded with small spikes (or 'thorns') beneath a garland of roses. She worked in her garden and sold the flowers she grew to help her family. In 1671, when asked to canonize her, Pope Clement X is said to have rejected the idea: 'What? An Indian saint? A shower of roses is just as likely!' Immediately roses rained down from heaven and threatened to inundate the Vatican. The Pope accepted the miracle and its implications, and the shower stopped. Rose is depicted with a rosary of thorns, surrounded by roses, or garlanded with them as she is borne to heaven by her divine Suitor.

The Rosary

The origin of the rosary is lost to us. It was probably oriental and came to the West in the ninth century. Pope Leo X approved its use in the early sixteenth century. Buddhists, Muslims and the Greek, Russian Orthodox and Roman Catholic Churches have rosaries with varying numbers of beads. The Catholic rosary has 165 beads, divided into fifteen sets of ten small beads each equivalent to an *Ave* or Hail Mary, and fifteen large beads, each standing for an Our Father and Glory be to the Father. The name comes from the Latin *rosarium*, a rose garden or rose bed, and the rosary is said to have begun as a wreath, garland or string of roses. *Rosarium* eventually became a term for the rosary itself. At some time in the West dried rose petals were crushed, moistened (possibly with rose water) and moulded into small beads to be dried, polished and threaded on a string, as they sometimes still are in the East. The word 'bead' itself comes from the Old English *gebed*, or prayer, and is directly derived from the equivalence of each bead counted to a prayer said.

The rosary is a garland of praise and a wreath of unity. It was known as the 'garden of our blessed Lady' and as the 'crown of Mary', and Our Lady of the Rosary is one of the titles of the Virgin Mary.[31] *Aves* became roses by a process of metaphorical derivation. Christ the Word was made flesh as a rose planted by the Divine Gardener in Mary's womb, a rose garden or new Paradise. Each 'Ave Maria' (consisting of five phrases and five petals standing for 'Maria', and thus a rose in itself) that we utter when meditating on this divine mystery echoes and acknowledges Jesus Christ the Word and Rose uttered and planted by God in Mary. Since antiquity a collection of fine poems or sayings had been known as an anthology (from the Greek *anthos*, a flower, and *logia*, a collection) or *florilegium*, for it was like a nosegay or posy. Collections of prayers and devotions came to be known as 'flower gardens' or 'gardens of the soul'. At some point in the Middle Ages, *rosarium* also came to designate an anthology of sacred poems or texts.

A perfectionist in a nineteenth-century convent trying to 'serve Our Lady in her garden' by reciting the rosary required a high degree of sophisticated mind-control, for she had to blend abstract thought with concrete detail in order to meditate simultaneously on an ineffable mystery and on an event in the life of Christ or Mary. Not surprisingly, in spite of her devotion to Our Lady, Thérèse found the repetitive prayers of the rosary more difficult to recite than wearing an 'instrument of penance'.[32] Nevertheless, as was the custom, she was buried with a rosary in her hand. When Dr La Néele wrote to her sister Léonie, on 10 September 1910, to describe the exhumation of Thérèse's body, he mentioned that the cross from her rosary was still in her fingers and that he had given it to Bishop Lemonnier as a souvenir.[33]

Roses and Blood

'The life of all flesh is the blood thereof', as the Bible reminds us (e.g. Lev. 17:14). Legends and beliefs among many peoples testify to the strengthening and fertilizing virtues of blood as the vehicle of the soul and of noble and generous impulses; to blood as the life-principle striving to survive after death as flower, plant or fruit; and to the association between blood and roses as promises of rebirth after sacrifice.[34] Roses grew from the blood of the dying god Adonis, and there are many accounts of wild roses springing from battlefields drenched in the blood of heroes, as after the victory at Roncesvalles when Charlemagne's knights died in defence of Christendom. In Christian symbolism a red rose stands for the blood of a martyr, and, by association with blood, may carry the symbolic attributes of fire, heat, sunlight and divine strength. The five-petalled rose signifies the five wounds of Christ, the blood flowing from them, and the resurrected life it promises us.

Thérèse passed through what has been called her dark night of the soul during a retreat (8–15 October 1896), when she told Father Godefroid Madelaine that she was troubled by severe doubts about her faith. He advised her always to carry a copy of the Creed next to her heart. To show her readiness to give her life for God she made the copy in her own blood.[35] She suffered and died from tuberculosis, the great scourge of the nineteenth and early twentieth centuries. The first signs of her impending death were apparent when she coughed up blood on Good Friday, 3 April 1896.[36] Roses have also come to stand for this feature of her disease and for the self-sacrificial aspects of her acceptance of pain and humiliation. Accordingly, many posthumous images show her holding the red roses of martyrdom.

Roses and Colours

As in secular life, so in the history of religion, red and white have signified various forms and instances of passion, love, suffering and purity. In one line of Jewish thought, the community of Israel is a rose, red in its strict and white in its tender aspect. In Christian tradition the interplay of red and white ranges from the Old Testament (Isaiah's 'though your sins are like scarlet, they shall be as white as snow; though they are red like crimson, they shall become like wool' [1:18], or the bride's declaration in the Song of Songs, 'My beloved is white and ruddy' [5:10, AV]), to the New (Revelation's son of man with head and hair 'white as snow' and eyes 'like a flame of fire' [1:14], or those who have made their robes 'white in the blood of the Lamb' [7:14]); from symbolic actions such as the seventh-century painting of Christ's tomb (according to the historian Bede) in a mixture of red and white, or St Bernard's 'The rose Mary was white for virginity, and red for love,' and the mystic Henry Suso's ardency and purity seen as a crown of red and white roses, all the way to the two dominant colours interwoven throughout Thérèse's writings.

She places more emphasis, however, on white than on red. White represents absolute purity of thought, endeavour and being. It is the sum of all colours, yet, as the absence of colour, beyond them. It is located before creation and the beginning of life, and after them. It is mystery at the heart of, yet also encompassing, the world of experience. It is the colour of virginity, candidacy, initiation, expectancy, submission and passivity before the intervention of passion, but also of revelation, transfiguration and rebirth thereafter. All colours are subsumed into the brilliant white halo or robe that stands for the experience and knowledge of God: 'And he was transfigured before them, and his clothes became dazzling white, such as no one on earth could bleach them' (Mark 9:2–5).

Thérèse was born in January, the month of white snow and ice. Her mother sold the delicate white lace known as *point d'Alençon*. Her favourite flowers were white roses, lilies, daisies and the tiny saxifrage.[37] Her first Communion dress and her novice's habit were white. On her robing day she interpreted a sudden fall of snow as a sign from God and was overjoyed to see snowflakes cover the courtyard and 'make it white like her'.[38] She all but identified herself with the colour white, and used it prolifically, beginning her autobiography with the 'Little white Flower' of the title and ending Manuscript A with a coat-of-arms in which she is Mary's white flower receiving the rays of the Morning Star. 'White', 'whiteness' and 'purity' recur throughout her letters to Céline, who would become a lily of 'dazzling whiteness' in heaven.[39]

Thérèse suffered and died from tuberculosis, known as the 'white death'.[40] The association with white continued after her death. She was photographed on her deathbed in the midst of white roses and lilies. When her relics were translated to Carmel on 26 March 1923 the coffin was draped in white, and the catafalque was drawn by four white horses ('greys', in equestrian circles), caparisoned in white and silver rugs, and with white plumes, bridles and reins.[41] Many testimonies by those who claimed to have seen Thérèse after her death described her as clad in white.

A Healing Flower

Throughout the ages a purifying quality has been ascribed to rose petals, hips, bark, roots and even dew gathered from the flower, which have provided perfumes, cosmetics and remedies for many afflictions, from nosebleeds to insanity. In the eighteenth century about one third of medicines used some part of the rose,[42] and many of these were still prescribed in the nineteenth century. Rose water has been used to purify sickrooms, temples, churches and streets.

The present-day use of the essential oil of the rose, the 'queen of flowers', in aromatherapy[43] reaches back to its distillation in tenth-century Persia, to the practice of the medieval alchemists for whom red and white roses had specific, even metaphysical, functions, and to the famous Nicholas Culpepper and herbalists of more recent centuries who recommended rose remedies (from a plant governed by Venus) for depression, melancholy, tension, for the skin, digestion and nervous system, but also as a stimulus to passion and conception.

For centuries *Rosa gallica officinalis*, the 'apothecary's rose', has been called on by herbalists to treat headaches, hysteria and other complaints, and would have been known to Thérèse's uncle, Isidore Guérin, a pharmacist who managed the Pierre Fournet pharmacy in Lisieux until 1888. He performed some of the functions of a guardian to the Martin daughters and was godfather to Pauline. It is not too fanciful to suppose that Thérèse would have gained some knowledge of healing from him and his family. After her death, a vast number of miracles of healing were attributed to Thérèse's intercession or her direct action, and the medical history and reputation of roses but also her emphasis on acceptance of illness and longing for spiritual wholeness and completion will have contributed to the intensity of faith and devotion that produced these results.

Thérèse's other Floral Images

In secular symbolism, wild and 'ordinary' flowers stand for childhood, simplicity, innocence, sincerity, an unpretentious, unspoiled nature and pristine virtue unsullied by artifice and commerce. They were especially cherished by Romantic writers and painters of the late eighteenth and the nineteenth century, for whom the pastoral figure of a child, particularly a girl, in a cottage garden or against a background of field flowers, represented an ideal to set against urban life and industrial production. Ruskin (much read in France, too, in Thérèse's lifetime) singled out Normandy, 'often rugged and covered with heather on the summits, and traversed by beautiful and singular dells, at once soft and secluded, fruitful and wild',[44] as an example of the beneficial influence of nature on religion and imaginative energy. He summarized the contemporary view of common wild flowers as neither 'degraded and distorted by any human interference', for they seem

> intended for the solace of ordinary humanity: children love them; quiet, tender, contented ordinary people love them as they grow; luxurious and disorderly people rejoice in them gathered. They are the cottager's treasure; and in the crowded town, mark, as with a little broken fragment of rainbow, the windows of the workers in whose heart rests the covenant of peace. Passionate or religious minds contemplate them with fond, feverish intensity. . . . To the child and the girl, the peasant and the manufacturing operative, to the grisette and the nun, the lover and monk, they are precious always. But to the men of supreme power and thoughtfulness, precious only at times . . .[45]

Although Thérèse is so often associated with roses, she frequently uses a small insignificant flower such as a violet, or a common or meadow wild flower such as a daisy, to convey the central point in what might be called her didactic mode (in other words, when she is teaching), and she often portrays herself as an ordinary little flower, planted and nurtured by Jesus in Mary's garden: 'Our Lady's Flower gathered such strength that five years later she unfolded her petals on the fertile mountain of Carmel.'[46] She also refers to Jesus and her Sisters in Carmel as wild flowers, and on one occasion in the same context. 'The Flower' was one of twenty-six poems (one for each member of the community) that made up Thérèse's fifth theatrical composition, 'The Holy Beggar-child at Christmas', inspired by a holy picture, 'From Crib to Calvary', which Sister Martha gave her on the day of her Profession (23 September 1890). She had planned the play as a quasi-liturgical ceremony. After the evening meal on Christmas Day the community knelt before the manger in order of precedence, the prioress first; picked a letter at random from a basket; then handed it to an angel (Sister Marie of the Eucharist), who sang the poem. Each Sister was invited to give Jesus something of herself – a smile, her heart, and so on – that responded symbolically to the Holy Child's request for alms. He asked not for 'good works' but for her love whole and entire. Whoever received the poem would meditate on its spiritual meaning:

> All the earth with snow is covered,
> Everywhere the white frosts reign;
> Winter and his gloomy servitors
> Hold their court on earth again.
> But for you has bloomed the Flower
> Of the fields, who comes to earth
> From the fatherland of heaven
> Where eternal spring has birth.
> Near the Rose of Christmas, Sister!
> In the lowly grasses hide,

> And be like the humble flowerets,
> Of heaven's King the lowly bride![47]

In the *Canticle of Céline*, in connection with love and her family, Thérèse evokes a range of vivid memories, sights and sounds of the countryside and nature from 'all the little flowers, buttercups so gentle', through 'the wheat fields and distant hills', 'the smell of roses', 'picking the heather', 'running on moss', catching 'butterflies fluttering on the ferns', the 'virgin forest with its mysterious flowers', to 'liana vines, periwinkles, hawthorn, fresh water lilies, honeysuckle and eglantine'.[48]

The following flowers and floral images are the most important of those referred to by Thérèse. This account of them does not pretend to be an exhaustive study of every flower mentioned in her works, but concentrates on their symbolic meaning for Thérèse and how that symbolism can bring our sensibility and understanding closer to the divine.

Aster (*aster tradescantia*)

The aster, or starwort, derives its name from the Greek word *aster* (star). In the language of flowers it is emblematical of an after-thought, a postscript, remembrance, or careful consideration, for it comes into bloom in October, when other flowers are scarce. Thérèse gave an aster to Céline every year to commemorate her feast day, which fell in that month. Thérèse calls it a 'Céline-flower', and she continued this family tradition in the convent by asking Céline to pick her own: 'P.S. Do not forget to pluck a little Céline-flower; it will be my heart offering it to you.'[49]

Cornflower (*centaurea cyanus*)

The cornflower signifies delicacy. The nuns remembered that the last flowers they gave Thérèse were cornflowers. She made two wreaths out of them, which she asked them to put in Mary's hands (that is, in those of the statue of Our Lady of Victories placed near Thérèse's bed in the infirmary), where they remained until Thérèse's death.[50]

Daisy (*bellis perennis*)

The daisy was also known as the love flower (*flos amoris*) or sun's consort (*sponsa solis*). A favourite of children and poets, it stands for innocence and contempt for worldly goods. The French word for daisy, *marguerite*, is derived from the Latin *margarita*, pearl, because the daisy's buds look like a row of pearls. For the Catholic Church the daisy, flowering in meadows with the onset of spring, not only tells us that Easter is imminent, but symbolizes the Virgin Mary and all-conquering love. Scattered throughout illustrations in books of hours, tiny daisies reminded the virtuous reader that they could learn something useful from even a single verse of Scripture or the liturgy as from the smallest flower in God's creation.

After studying the daisy-pinned meadow at Carmel that some members of the community had wanted to uproot,[51] Thérèse wrote to Céline on 26 April 1892, enclosing as a symbolic gift a daisy that had been held by Mother Genevieve (foundress and prioress of the convent at Lisieux), who died on 5 December 1891:

> One day, amid the grass all white with single daisies, I thought I saw one with a slender stalk, more beautiful than the rest; coming close, I saw with surprise that it was not one daisy, but two quite distinct ones. Two stalks so closely united reminded me at once of the mysteries of *our souls*. . . . I realized that if, in nature, it pleases Jesus to sow marvels so entrancing beneath our feet, it is only to aid us to glimpse the mysteries, more hidden and of a higher order, that he sometimes works in souls . . . .

To rejoice our eyes and instruct our souls, Jesus has created a multitude of little daisies. In the morning I see with wonder that their rosy petals are turned toward the dawn, they are waiting for the sun to rise. The moment that radiant star casts one of its warm beams upon them, the shy little flowers begin to open their calyces, and their tiny petals form a sort of crown, which lets you see through to their little yellow hearts and thus gives these flowers a strong resemblance to the being which has touched them with its light. All through the day, the daisies never take their gaze from the sun, turning with him until evening; then, when he has disappeared, they quickly fold up their petals and from white become rosy again. . . . Jesus is the Divine Sun and the daisies are his brides, the Virgins . . .

In his meadow Jesus has many daisies, but they are separate and each receives separately the rays of the sun. One day the Spouse of Virgins bent down upon the earth, bound two little barely opened buds tight together, their stalks were fused into a single stalk, and under a single gaze they grew. Together these little flowers, now *one single flower*, blossomed; and now the double daisy fixing its gaze upon its Divine Sun carries out its own unique mission. . . . To the eye of creatures our lives seem very different, totally separate, but I know that Jesus has bound our hearts together in so marvellous a fashion that whatever makes the one heart beat sets the other vibrating too.

The same gaze ravished our souls, a gaze dimmed with tears which the double daisy has resolved to dry; its humble white petals will be the chalice in which those precious diamonds will be collected to be poured in turn upon other flowers, less privileged flowers, which have not fixed their hearts' first gaze on Jesus.[52]

Oxeye daisy (*chrysantheum leucanthemum*)

Legends say that it bloomed in front of the manger when Christ was born.

Forget-me-not (*myosotis scorpiodes*)

The forget-me-not has small, delicate blue blossoms that look like eyes. It is also known as 'myosotis', from the Greek for 'mouse's ear', because the tiny, elegant leaves resemble the ears of mice. It is the flower of remembrance par excellence, not only of individuals but of one's obscurity, insignificance and fragility.

The forget-me-not was the favourite flower of Sister Marie of the Trinity. On 30 April 1896, when Marie took her vows, her novice mistress, Thérèse, covered her charge's bed with forget-me-nots (one name for the flower in the past was 'Mary's bed-straw') and wrote an accompanying note: 'I should like to have flowers that will not die to give you in memory of this beautiful day, but it is only in heaven that flowers will never fade.'[53] She developed the symbolism in another letter, over a year later, to explain that no rigorous scrutiny was necessary to see Marie's humility, and that she should not abase herself by neglecting to receive Communion in supposed reparation for an oversight:

> Dear little flower beloved of Jesus . . . the *tiny eye* in your calyx shows me what to think of the whole little flower. . . . I am very pleased, very much consoled, but you must no longer *want* to *eat* earth; the forget-me-not need only open, or rather upraise its calyx for the Bread of Angels to come like a divine Dew to strengthen it and to give it all that it lacks. . . . Good night, poor flowerlet, take my word that I love you more than you think![54]

Lily (*lilium candidum*)

The lily carries a multitude of associations in literature, art and religion. It is the flower of exalted and unapproachable rank or virtue. The white Madonna lily was an emblem of Mary for centuries, for the petals represent her physical purity and the

golden anthers symbolize her spiritual purity; it can grow to a
height of 1.5 metres (5 feet). It was thought to reflect pure
light and therefore stands for unassailable or perfect innocence
and virginity. In Scripture, the lily signifies divine election, as
of Israel among the nations: 'As a lily among brambles, so is
my love among maidens' (Song of Songs, 2:2), and God's
concern for his elect: 'Consider the lilies of the field, how they
grow; they neither toil nor spin' (Matthew 6:28). When they
let themselves fall into God's hands and are thereby clothed
with his grace, 'even Solomon in all his glory was not arrayed
like one of these' (ibid.) Similarly, the lily symbolizes the
Immaculate Conception of Our Lady. In Thérèse's poem to St
Cecilia, in several letters to Céline, and elsewhere, the lily
stands for the ideal condition of a virginal bride of Christ. In
'A Crown of Lilies' she portrayed lilies as the souls who had
chosen and were chosen to compose Christ's crown:

> Sinners will crown with thorns one day
> The holy, heavenly head of Christ.
> What pains and sorrows will be his,
> To gain us graces all unpriced.
> Now may your virginal sweet soul
> Make him tonight his woes forget;
> And for his royal lily-crown
> Your Sisters' souls before him set.
> Draw very close to Jesus' throne,
> And charm his lovely tear-dimmed eyes;
> Make with these virgin souls his crown
> Of snow-white lilies beyond price.[55]

Thérèse also painted a chasuble (modelled on the painting
on parchment by her sister Pauline of 27 April 1890, given to
Céline on her twenty-first birthday). It showed the Holy Face
among roses and lilies representing Mr and Mrs Martin and

their children. The two white roses at the base of the cross were her father and mother; the five lilies around the Holy Face were their five daughters; and Thérèse identified herself as the lily half-obscured by the veil of St Veronica. The four lily buds symbolized her four brothers and sisters who died in infancy.[56]

Not only because they stood for mystical abandonment to divine grace and God's predestined choice, but because of their powerful fragrance, lilies were often favoured as flowers of and for the dead. Photographs of Thérèse on her deathbed show her crowned with lilies.

Fleur-de-lys (*iris pseudocorus; iris germanica*)

The fleur-de-lys (or fleur-de-lis) is the emblem of the French monarchy, and a sceptre tipped with a fleur-de-lys is the attribute of the archangel Gabriel, especially at the Annunciation. The device was associated with Joan of Arc because of her defence of the divinely chosen King of France and of the sanctity of the realm under God. Joan was one of Thérèse's heroines, and she wore a dress imprinted with fleur-de-lys when playing Joan of Arc in the dramatic piece she had written about the Saint.[57] The emblem also appeared on floor-tiles in her childhood home in Alençon.

Lily of the valley (*convallaria majalis*)

Its minute bell-shaped flowers often look like tears and have supported its citation as a flower of sorrow and compassion. Traditionally, the lily of the valley signifies simplicity, innocence and unadorned candour, or happiness regained. In a religious context it is a pure soul, or one infused with grace. In Christian symbolism it is Christ himself or a Christ-like soul. In one line of Christian reinterpretation of the symbolism of the Song of Songs (Song of Solomon) the valley is the world and the lily Christ. The lily of the valley is also associated with the tree of life that grows in the Garden of Paradise, and signifies the spotless life to which we in the world of sin and exile can always look as a sure promise of redemption and transfiguration. For Thérèse, Christ as the Lily of the valley is Jesus as he chose to manifest himself on earth 'solely to show us how he loves simplicity'.[58]

In her letters to Céline, particularly, that of 25 April 1893, Thérèse observed that the distinctive quality of Céline's heart was simplicity and that she should not seek to emulate garden (that is, cultivated) flowers, for Jesus referred to himself as the 'flower of the fields, the lily of the valleys' (cf. Song of Songs 2:1, Matt. 6.28–30). But when Jesus the lily of these valleys became transfigured as the 'Sun of Justice', and revealed himself as the 'glowing furnace of uncreated Love', then Céline, a little flower in imitation of him, having become his dewdrop, would ascend like a 'light vapour' together with Thérèse until both were distilled by the same ray of love and were 'united for eternity in the heart of the Divine Sun'.[59]

Palm (*phoenix dactylifera*)

The early church adopted the palm, a processional symbol of military victory, as a symbol of Christ's, and therefore a Christian's, conquest of death (cf. Rom. 6:9–10). It stands for resurrection and immortality, and may also signify the soul itself. Thérèse uses it in this sense, but pre-eminently as the palm of the martyrs: 'But nothing is too much to suffer to win the palm.'[60] Her poem of missionary enthusiasm addressed to Our Lady of Victories says: 'The palm my spirit longs to gain, / My brother's hand in mine shall place. / A martyr's sister! Any pain / Would seem delight to win that grace.'[61]

Thérèse was buried with a palm found to be in perfect condition when her coffin was exhumed on 6 September 1910.

Reed (*phragmites australis; phragmites communis*)

In Scripture the reed stands for weakness; the water can shake it and the wind bend it: 'the Lord will smite Israel, as a reed is shaken in the water' (1 Kings 14:15). In French it is *roseau*, one of a number of terms semantically and lyrically associated with the rose and forming a set of references played on symbolically, as by Thérèse, but quite lost in English translation. In accordance with a well-known observation of Blaise Pascal, the great French seventeenth-century philosopher and scientist (in his *Pensées*), a human being is only a reed, the weakest known to nature, but a thinking reed ('roseau pensant'), and therefore strong in awareness of the existence of which nature is unconscious.

For her robing ceremony, Thérèse received a reed as the distinctive emblem for her clothing. This was customary in the Lisieux Carmel, where emblems were used in preference to numbers. She depicted herself as a weak reed in her coat-of-arms. In a letter to Sister Marie of the Sacred Heart (12–20 May 1888), she referred to herself as a weak little reed, which could bend with the slightest breeze; she signed a letter to Sister Agnes of Jesus (Pauline) (4 July 1888) 'The little Reed of Jesus', and continued the symbolic theme in the following letter: 'Sometimes small puffs of wind are more insupportable to the *reed* than great storms; for in the storms it is bowed down to soak in the stream that it loves, but the small puffs of wind do not bend it so low. They are the pinpricks.'[62]

Saxifrage

The drooping saxifrage (*saxifraga cernua*) or the fingered or rue-leaved saxifrage (*saxifraga tridactylites*) grows on old walls and rocks, and in dry, sandy ground. It has white flowers only 4–6 mm in diameter, appearing in loose clusters or alone. It flowers from June to September. Thérèse's father plucked a saxifrage from a wall when she announced that she was going to become a nun.[63] In one sense, it is this particular flower she is thinking of when she portrays herself as a little white flower in the opening pages of her autobiography. At the same time it symbolizes her desire to be no more than a simple wild flower in accordance with her 'Little Way'. She also describes herself as preceded and surrounded by eight lilies (her family). Because the saxifrage is also a 'miniature lily', as she explains, she is also one of the 'branch of lilies' who would soon be together in heaven.[64]

Violet (*viola odorata*)

The violet stands for modesty and humility. In Christian tradition it is associated with Christ's earthly life, usually as an infant, though it sometimes appears at the foot of the cross in paintings of the Crucifixion. For Thérèse, the violet or its unassuming scent represents yet another variety of simplicity:

> The brilliance of the rose and the whiteness of the lily do not lessen the perfume of the violet or the sweet simplicity of the daisy. . . . He has also created lesser ones, who must be content to be daisies or simple violets flowering at his feet, and whose mission is to gladden his divine eyes.[65]

The scent or manifestation of violets is often reported by people who claim to have been helped by Thérèse. In the 1920s Lucie Delarue-Mardrus interviewed the caretaker of a chateau near Lisieux:

> 'In Lisieux they say there was throughout the convent, after her death, a perfume of violets . . . I don't know about that; I smelt nothing then. But there are others who did.'
> 'Violets? I should think roses, rather!'
> 'Oh! No, Madame! It was the same when they took her body

from the ground. They write now in the books that her body smelt of roses. But it was violets. And anyway, the violet is much more like Sister Thérèse, who was so modest.'[66]

Wheat (corn) (*triticum aestivum*)

Wheat stands for abundance. Thérèse told Céline that one day she was wondering how to save souls and remembered that Jesus had said: 'The harvest indeed is great, but the labourers are few. Pray ye therefore, the Lord of the harvest that He send forth labourers.' She knew, however, that: 'Our own vocation . . . is not to go harvesting in the fields of ripe corn; Jesus does not say to us: "Lower your eyes, look at the fields and go reap them." Our mission is still loftier.'[67]

Near the end of her life someone brought her a sheaf of corn. She picked the most beautiful one and said that the ear of corn was the image of her soul, for God had entrusted her with graces for herself and for many others.[68]

White mignonette (*reseda alba*)

In the nineteenth-century language of flowers, the white mignonette signified 'Your qualities surpass your charms.' It flowers from June to August. On 25 August 1885, the feast of St Louis of France, Thérèse sent her father, Louis Martin, who was visiting the Balkans, a letter decorated with a flower sewn to it and encircled by the words: 'Reseda picked in my garden.'[69]

Calyx (pl. calyces)

The 'calyx' is the collective term for the sepals of a flower, the bract-like growth that protects the bud before it opens. In ancient symbolism it is the receptacle of heavenly action, of divinities that manifest themselves as rain or dew. In French *calice* means both 'calyx' and 'chalice', and therefore has an obvious religious association lost in English but deliberately invoked in Thérèse's writings. When she describes her first Communion, she is Our Lady's little flower, and her calyx protects her as Mary's cloak protected Jesus; it is also the chalice that, paradoxically, miraculously, receives him. Then the greater Flower, 'Flower of the fields and Lily of the valley', chooses to become a little flower even smaller than Thérèse, and allows his mother to place him in Thérèse's humble protection just as he descends into the Communion cup.[70]

A similarly profound mystery is enacted within an insignificant flower, in the calyx-chalice of the soul:

> The eyes of creatures do not bother to pause upon a little *Céline-flower*, yet its white cup is full of mystery. It has in its heart a great number of other flowers, which are of course the children of its *soul* (souls); and then its white calyx is red within. As though it were stained with its blood! . . . Céline, the sun and the rain can fall upon this little insignificant flower and do not wither it. No one thinks to pick it, so it stays virgin. . . . Yes, for Jesus alone has seen it, it was he who created it, and for himself alone! Oh! But then it is more fortunate than the glowing rose which is not for Jesus alone.[71]

A year later Thérèse wrote again to her Aster, her 'dear little flower', to expand the imagery of the calyx-chalice of the fruitful soul, where virtue breeds virtue, enclosing not merely flowers but a vast number of other calyces producing honey not to be guarded jealously for its own sake but released, without questioning the purpose, to Jesus for his mysterious purposes before the winter of death makes all these treasures of suffering and self-denial so many accusations of waste. The message is that Céline-flowers that fester smell far worse than weeds:

> Only the bees know the treasures enclosed in its mysterious calyx, composed of a multitude of small calyces all equally

rich. . . . Jesus and the angels . . . who like the bees, know how to gather the honey contained in those many mysterious calyces, which stand for the souls, or rather the children, of the virginal little flower.[72]

Corolla

Thérèse followed her prize-book, Chaudé's *Theology of Plants* (see above, p. 14) in assigning to the corolla (all a flower's petals considered together) the status of 'empress of the vegetal world . . . proclaiming the hand of God':

In the morning I see with wonder that their rosy corollas are turned toward the dawn, they are waiting for the sun to rise. The moment that radiant star casts one of its warm beams upon them, the shy little flowers begin to open their calyces, and their tiny petals form a sort of crown, which lets you see through to their little yellow hearts and thus gives these flowers a strong resemblance to the being which has touched them with light. All through the day, the daisies never take their gaze from the sun, turning with him until evening; then, when he has disappeared, they quickly fold up their corollas and from white become rosy again.[73]

In her long poem, 'Remember, Jesus my Beloved', corollas are those flowers who sacrifice their lives and, raised to the point of intensity, respond to God's love as his helpers in the gathering of the final harvest:

Your blood, your tears, a fruitful living source,
Make these corollas virginal, not poor;
And to them grant a wondrous, holy force,
For winning souls to serve you and adore.

> A virginal heart is mine; yet, profoundly true!
> Mother of souls I am, through my chaste bond with you,
> To these virgin flowers that bloom
> Only to bring poor sinners home.[74]

Dew

In Latin languages there is a close semantic connection between the rose, the colour pink (Latin *roseus-a-um*, French *rose*), and dew, moisture, and a refreshing rainfall (Latin *ros*, French *rosée*), and related words, such as 'sprinkle' (French *arroser*), which is quite lost in English. The term 'pink' came into use in English as synonymous with 'roseate', 'rose-coloured', 'rosy', and so on, only in the early nineteenth century, but gradually replaced those rose adjectives in normal discourse. This affects English versions of Thérèse's writings, which necessarily obscure the lyrical and intended associations between roses, pink and dew in the original texts, and especially the symbolism of regeneration and initiation into life-giving mystery attributed to the flower and to the colour by virtue of this connection with dew, moisture and rain. 'Rosée' (dew) in devotional writing also suggests heavenly grace ('For your dew is a radiant dew, and the earth will give birth to those long dead' (Isaiah 26:19), pearls of divine blessing, and the drops of redemptive blood falling from Christ's wounds. Each of these drops, in medieval and baroque iconography and the tradition inherited from it, is also or produces a rose petal. There are similar associations in French verse. An attenuated version of this system of correspondences, which extended the field of meaning of the word 'rose', was a firm part of Thérèse's thinking, and of her national, linguistic and religious culture.

The word '*rosée*' (dew) appears at least fifty times in Thérèse's writings. It was a richly significant term for so keen an observer of her natural surroundings. In her autobiography, when describing the period just after her mother's death, she remarked that if Jesus had not 'lavished his sunshine upon his Little Flower, she never could have become acclimatised to this earth. Still too weak to bear the rain or storm, she needed warmth, refreshing dew, and gentle breezes – gifts never denied her, even in the wintry season of trials.'[75]

In 1889 Céline had written a poem entitled 'Dew' ('La Rosée'), which Thérèse liked so much that she had learned some passages by heart.[76] Her letters to Céline often rely on dew symbolism. This is especially true of one of 25 April 1893 in which the word '*rosée*' appears twenty times, and Céline must 'remain *a drop of dew* hidden in the divine cup of the lovely Lily of the Valleys'.[77]

Thérèse's first poem, 'The Divine Dew, or The Virginal Milk of Mary', was written on 2 February 1893 at the insistence of Sister Teresa of St Augustine, who asked for an explanation of Jesus' infancy. Thérèse's sources were a passage from Guéranger's *Liturgical Year* and some excerpts from St Augustine. She added her own imagery of the flower, blood, the rose and dew to illustrate a difficult doctrine. Much as her name in religion, Sister Thérèse of the Child Jesus and the Holy Face, combined the ideas of Christ's birth and Passion, so she used dew as a metaphor to unite the Incarnation and the eucharistic Passion: 'Your dew is Virginal Milk' and 'Your divine blood is Virginal Milk!' A rosebud unfurls under the rays of the sun and is nourished by fresh drops of morning dew, just as the infant Jesus is cradled in Mary's arms:

> Those spotless pearls of clear translucent dew
> Are full of some mysterious power;
> They form the sap then vitally renew
> And open petals of the half-blown flower.

You are the Flower with petals still unclosed;
I gaze upon your beauty undefiled.
You are the Rose of Sharon long foretold,
Still in your glorious bud, you heavenly Child!
Your dearest mother's arms, so pure and white,
Now make for you a royal cradle-throne;
Your morning sun is Mary's bosom bright,
Your sunlit dew her virginal milk, my Own![78]

Thérèse often invoked the traditional use of dew (*rosée*) as a metaphor for the blood of Jesus, and in her poems and elsewhere extended its symbolism to Jesus' tears of blood:

Remember your dread hour of agony
When blood and tears bore witness to your woe.
Dew-pearls of love, rubies so fair to see,
From which blooms of virginal beauty grow.
An angel showed the harvest you would reap,
Bringing gladness then, although you must weep.
And truly you could see,
Among those lilies, me![79]

Thérèse had a burning desire to save souls for God. After reading in *La Croix* that, moments before his execution, the murderer Pranzini had kissed Jesus' wounds three times, Thérèse was convinced that her prayers on his behalf had been answered. From then on her longing to save souls increased daily. She felt that Jesus was whispering to her as he had to the Samaritan woman when he asked her for water: 'It was truly an exchange of love: I poured out the Precious Blood of Jesus upon souls, and that I might quench his thirst, I offered to Jesus these same souls refreshed with the dew of Calvary.'[80]

She prayed constantly for the flowers of humanity to grow to fullness through the dew of redemption:

You, Lord, know well my soul's most ardent prayer:
I long to give you this Earth's lilies fair;
Spring buds for you, my Lily so adored.
Baptize each one with dew, then pluck them, Lord.[81]

Perfume

In Catholic liturgy and devotion, perfume as of the sweetest flowers is offered actually and metaphorically in honour of the divine fragrance ('his beauty shall be like the olive, and his fragrance like Lebanon', Hosea 14:6), just as in the ancient world essential oils were extracted and mixed and incense was offered in temples in honour of the all-surpassing perfume of gods and goddesses. The subtlety of a perfume is like the uniqueness of a human soul. Each flower has its variously persistent scent, and each person a spiritual presence that lingers though the body withers. Perfume is cleansing, purifying and illuminative: 'Each plant is a lamp, and its perfume light' (Victor Hugo). According to Thérèse, we are flowers waiting for God's all-powerful fragrance to call forth each singular perfume, as love responds to the action of Love: 'His divine blood flows out upon our petals and his thorns tear us so that the perfume of our love can breathe forth.'[82]

In a poem to Mother Marie de Gonzague on her sixtieth birthday, Thérèse described her as Jesus' 'sweet-smelling flower'.[83]

She told Céline later that year:

The most fervent *Christians*, the *priests*, consider that we are *too extreme*, that we ought to *serve* with Martha instead of consecrating to Jesus the *vessels* of our *lives* with the perfumes contained in them . . . but after all, does it matter that our *vessels* are broken, since Jesus is *consoled*, and since, in spite of itself, the world is forced to *awareness* of the perfumes they emit, which serve to purify the poisoned air the world is always breathing.[84]

All the associations of Thérèse's flowers, from the purity and passion of roses white and red aspiring to fulfilment in the garden of the ultimate Rose, to the dew-fed loveliness of lilies elicited by the fairest Lily of the Valley, are summarized in the image of their perfume:

> 'To live by love, what foolishness she sings!'
> So cries the world. 'Renounce that idle joy!
> Don't waste your perfumes on such trivial things.
> Your life and gifts in useful arts employ!'
> To love you, Jesus! Ah, that loss is gain.
> For my perfumes I seek no praise, but fly
> From this world now, singing in sweetest pain:
> 'Of love I die!'[85]

and:

> Your Face is now my fatherland,
> The radiant sunshine of my days,
> My realm of love, my sunlit land,
> Where, all life long, I sing your praise.
> It is the Lily of the vale,
> Whose mystic perfume, freely given,
> Brings comfort, when I faint and fail,
> And lets me taste the peace of heaven.[86]

Thérèse devoted the last words of the unfinished Manuscript C to a similarly graphic illustration of all that she meant by the 'sweet odour of the Beloved' refreshing and drawing his flowers to him. Since Jesus was in heaven, she said, she could follow him only by keeping to the star-pattern which he inscribed on the darkness of life, and by following the traces of light and fragrance which he had left behind him: 'As soon as I open the Holy Gospels I breathe the perfume exhaled by the life of Jesus, and I know which way to run.'[87]

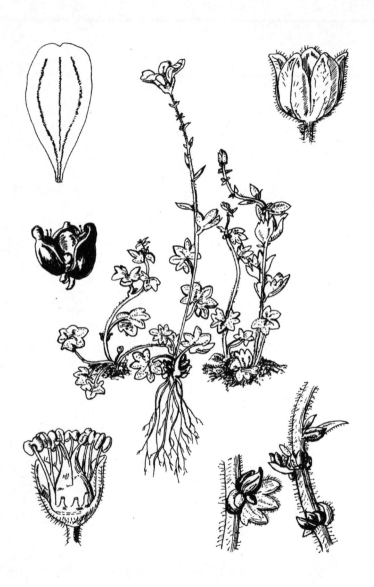

❧ 2 ❧

1873–1888

The rose that with your earthly eyes you see / Has flowered in God from all eternity.

Angelus Silesius

In the season of roses the trees speak softly of love.

Victor Hugo

Again and again I have noticed that all through my life nature has reflected my feelings.

Thérèse of Lisieux

Thérèse's religious and aesthetic sensibility was nourished by the zeal and aspirations of her parents. Both Louis and Marie-Azélie had wanted to enter the religious life but, for different reasons, had been rejected by their chosen Orders. This longing was so intense that initially their married life was that of two celibates, like St Cecilia and Valerian.

Louis-Joseph-Aloys-Stanislaus Martin was born in Bordeaux on 22 August 1823. His father was a captain in the army and a devout Catholic. He moved his family to Avignon, then Strasbourg and, when he retired, to his native Normandy.

Louis was sensitive, mystical and artistic, though somewhat melancholy, and did not follow his father in a military career. He spent a year (1842–3) with a cousin in Rennes, where he took up clock- and watch-making. This intricate work suited his desire for silence and the opportunity to meditate. He was

largely self-educated. During his technical training he filled
two thick notebooks with quotations from a wide selection of
classical and modern authors. The seventeenth-century theo-
logian and moralist Fénelon, whose treatise on the existence
of God sought proofs for it in the wonders of the natural
world, was one of Louis' favourite spiritual writers. Among
the Romantics he preferred Lamartine and Chateaubriand,
who introduced him to the cult of nature: 'the sonorous lam-
entations of . . . romantic melancholies re-echoing through
the world and eternity'.[1] He found the 'oak-covered, granite
land' and folklore of Brittany most congenial. Like Rousseau's 'solitary stroller' (of the *Rêveries d'un Promeneur
Solitaire*), he enjoyed walking in dramatic landscapes, which
assured his spirit that the present was a perpetual moment in
which it lacked nothing, although for Louis this meant that
they raised his mind and heart to God. In 1843 he made a
pilgrimage to the Hospice of Mont-Joux, the famous Great St
Bernard monastery, in Switzerland, where he hoped to
become a monk. He kept a small flower as a memento of this
visit and of his intention. It was preserved in the family
records and was probably in his mind as, years later, he plucked
a white saxifrage from a wall when Thérèse said she wanted
to enter the Lisieux Carmel. For the Martins, the language
of flowers was an important way of expressing their most
cherished ideals and, like most people then, they used
pressed flowers to mark and recall significant occasions.

Louis went back to Mont-Joux two years later but was
rejected because he had no Latin. He returned to Alençon to
continue his studies, but ill health forced him to abandon all
hopes of the religious life. Eventually he opened a jewellery
and clock- and watch-making business and worked hard at his
craft. Otherwise he was reclusive and bought a hexagonal
tower, known as 'the Pavilion', as a 'retreat' near the River
Sarthe in the southern part of Alençon. Louis turned this into

an austere shrine where he kept a few spiritual books and his fishing tackle. He planted the surrounding land with flowers and a walnut tree.

His future wife, Marie-Azélie (or Zélie) Martin Guérin, born on 23 December 1831, was a Norman. She had an older sister, Marie-Louise, who later became a nun at the Visitation Convent in Le Mans, and a younger brother, Isidore. Zélie's health was very delicate and she suffered from constant headaches, possibly induced by her parents' severity and misunderstanding of her sensitive nature, so that her childhood and youth were 'shrouded in sadness'.

Zélie was educated by Sacred Heart nuns in Alençon. She wanted to consecrate her life to God and become a Vincentian nun, but was refused entry because of her health. Instead she mastered the intricate art of *point d'Alençon* lace-making, and from 1853 ran a very successful business from her parents' house. Her devotion to her sister Marie-Louise, the 'soul of her soul', was a model for that of Thérèse to her sister Céline. Marie-Louise's entry to the Le Mans convent distressed Zélie deeply, and cannot have been without affect on Zélie's marriage to Louis Martin on 13 July 1858, only a few months later. The couple visited Marie-Louise at Le Mans on their wedding day but, as Zélie told her daughter Pauline later, this only reminded her of the peace and calm she had dreamed of. Her husband comforted her 'for he had similar inclinations. I even think that our mutual affection was increased.'[2]

Their confessor persuaded Louis and Zélie to change their attitude to marriage after ten months of celibacy. They realized that, to some extent, they could fulfil their own unrealized religious vocations by bringing up their children to dedicate their lives to God. They were to have nine of them over thirteen years. Zélie had become 'madly fond of children'. She was forty-one and Louis in his late forties when Thérèse, their last child, was born. Zélie decided to have no more. She was almost morbidly preoccupied with death, for she had lost four children, and Marie, Pauline, Léonie and Céline were thirteen, twelve, ten, and four years old. She was also tired out by long hours of lace-making, business affairs, running a family, and charitable works.

Budding: 2 January 1873–2 October 1881

Thérèse's association with flowers began just after her birth when a small boy knocked on the Martins' door and handed the parents a poem by a man befriended and helped by Louis and Zélie Martin after he had fallen on hard times. It contained the prediction: 'Yes, bud newly opened, smile at the dawn, / You, little bud, will be a rose one morn.'[3] By the end of January, however, Thérèse was suffering from gastroenteritis, the illness that had killed four of her siblings. After a month the doctor said a wet nurse must be found or Thérèse would die. Zélie contacted Rosalie Taillé, a wet nurse to the family in the past and known to them affectionately as 'Little Rose'. She was still breast-feeding her youngest child, aged thirteen months. Thérèse was sent to Rosalie's simple thatched house in Semallé, a small village a few miles to the north of Alençon, lived as a peasant baby for just over a year, and became plump and healthy. Rosalie took her about perched on bundles of grass in a wheelbarrow. Her awakening consciousness received impressions of meadows and flowers, the smells of the farmyard and new-mown hay, the scrabbling of chickens and cockerels, and the lowing of Redskin, the family cow.

Once a week Rosalie went to Alençon market to sell her farm produce, and took Thérèse to see her mother, who wrote several times to her sister-in-law describing Thérèse's attachment to Rosalie, to whose stall she had to be taken when she had been left at home but would not stop crying. At the beginning of April 1874 the fourteen-month-old Thérèse had to make a difficult adjustment by exchanging four surrogate brothers for four sisters, and the life of a country peasant for a bourgeois town existence. For some time she would cry if she saw Rosalie passing the window on her way to market, and Semallé became the verdant paradise of infancy that she never forgot. During her first year in Carmel, she recalled what she had surrendered: 'Never again shall I see cornflowers, tall daisies, corn-poppies, oats or wheat.'[4]

Céline and Marie, too, were fond of Rosalie. Céline wrote (12–17 April 1877) to her first cousin, Jeanne Guérin, to describe their visit to 'Little Rose', and how they drank milk, played wolf, climbed trees and made a swing. Marie said their happiest holiday experience was to visit Rose, and that she was enchanted by the fields of wheat studded with daisies, cornflowers and poppies.[5] Similar images of the Norman countryside may be traced in Louise Swanton Belloc's *Le Sentier d'Or*, a story that greatly impressed the young Thérèse and contributed to her imagery of earth and heaven as flower gardens: one spoiled and inadequate, the other a fully-realized and perfect domain. The heroine dreams that she sails along the Path of Gold formed by the reflection of the setting sun on the sea, before stepping ashore on a magical land shaded by magnificent trees and filled with flowers and birds she has never seen nor heard before: 'The air was pure, light, balmy; just as she reached it, as she put her little foot on the soft and flowery lawn . . . she woke up.'[6]

Thérèse's family was warm and loving. Her first memories were full of smiles and tender caresses. She was a gifted child, assessed as very intelligent and advanced for her age, and extremely sensitive, but with a very determined will which her mother characterized as stubborn.

The family's existence was centred on their Catholic faith. Although engaged in business, Louis and Zélie saw worldly goods as reflecting heavenly goods and conceived of their lives as a quest for another world: this was the true fatherland from which Thérèse and her sisters were exiled and to which they must always aspire.

Louis' love of fishing and retreats into the countryside were in the same order of dedication as his frequent pilgrimages, and they fostered Thérèse's love of her natural surroundings as a foretaste of heaven. To accompany her father to his pavilion was a treat, and, even though the children were encouraged to take an interest in the geraniums and dahlias in their Alençon garden, Thérèse adored the Sunday walks with her mother in the countryside. There wild flowers, sunny cornfields, clumps of trees round farms set at long intervals, and vistas reaching to the edges of distant forests under skies stained by the changing colours of the day, were fresh and liberating compared with the close streets of their town and its symmetrical flower beds:

> I can still feel the vivid and poetic impressions made on my childish heart by the vision of the cornfields studded with cornflowers, poppies, and marguerites. Even at that age I loved far-stretching views, sunlit spaces, and stately trees: in a word all the beauties of nature cast their spell upon me and raised my soul to heaven.[7]

From a very early age, the sensitive Thérèse learned to associate flowers, gardens and love with death and self-sacrifice. Even before cancer was confirmed as the cause of Zélie's sickness, and quite apart from the children she had lost, the family constantly referred to death in the style of Christian devotion of a period much obsessed with it. Zélie was very keen on reading and talking about the lives of appropriate saints. In 1876, when Thérèse was three, her mother was immersed in the biography of St Françoise Romaine. Zélie found Françoise especially attractive because she had asked one of many apparitions of her dead son if he was thinking of her and loved her. The visitant assured her that in heaven one was completely absorbed in God and had no pain. Around this time, too, a new gardener delighted the children with stories of dead people. Not long before, Zélie had written to Pauline, at the boarding school in Le Mans attached to the Visitation convent where Zélie's sister was a nun, to tell her how Thérèse had hugged her, said how much she hoped her mother would die because then she would be in heaven, and had shown her affection for her father in the same way. But self-sacrifice was more difficult to accept. After one walk, Thérèse was busy making flowers she had gathered into bunches. Grandmother Martin picked out the best bouquet and claimed it for her private altar. Céline noticed the tears in Thérèse's eyes, but the flowers had to be surrendered.

The family's happiness was soon clouded. For Thérèse a pleasingly vague concept became immediate reality. In December 1876, Zélie, unwilling to worry Louis or her children with her health, finally consulted a doctor about the reappearance of a tumour on her breast. It was too late for palliative measures. On 24 February 1877 she received a further blow when her sister, Sister Marie Dorothée, died. In spite of a wearing pilgrimage to Lourdes, the cancer developed rapidly and Zélie died too. When Thérèse recalled this harsh childhood loss and being held up to kiss her mother's 'icy forehead', she typically used floral imagery to interpret her ordeal in a meaningful context: 'As early spring flowers begin to come up under the snow and open at the first rays of the sun, so the Little Flower ... had to pass through the winter of trial and have her delicate cup filled with the dew of tears.'[8]

Thérèse did not show great emotion at her mother's death, but the effects were profound. She became sad, shy and extra-sensitive; burst into tears at a look from a stranger; and was at ease only with her family:

If our Lord had not lavished his sunshine upon his Little Flower, she never could have become acclimatized to this earth. Still too weak to bear either rain or storm, she needed warmth, refreshing dew, and gentle breezes – gifts never denied her, even in the wintry season of trials.[9]

Before she died Madame Martin had asked her brother, Isidore Guérin (later deputy guardian to his nieces), to find a house for the family near him in Lisieux. She asked expressly for a big garden, or at least a plot where the children could plant flowers. In November the Martin family moved into a 'delightful house topped by a belvedere' which the children named 'Les Buissonnets', a more euphonious derivation from 'des Bissonnets' – the name of the district itself. At the front there was a small landscaped garden bordered by shrubs, and at the rear a spacious garden with massive yucca trees on the lawn, a shed, laundry, greenhouse and shelter for poultry and rabbits, and another enclosure and shelter for ducks.

Thérèse's experience of her new home was blissful. The lawn, kitchen garden and view 'appealed to my young imagination. Its situation . . . added charm, for it stood in a quiet part of the town, within easy reach of a beautiful park laid out with flowers . . . my little heart expanded and I smiled on life once more'.[10] The Jardin de l'Etoile, the park behind the cathedral, was a special grace. Subscribers were allowed to pick some flowers and it became one of Thérèse's favourite spots.

Lisieux was set in a pleasant valley, the meeting-place of one very small river, the Cirieux, and the larger Orbec and Touques. It was surrounded by pastureland and gentle hills. Apple trees for making Calvados, the Norman spirit, flourished at roadsides and in fields as well as orchards. Lisieux's wealth was based on various textile factories, a cotton mill, tanneries and its market; it was also a garrison town. Marcel Proust in his great novel-sequence, *Remembrance of Times Past (À la Recherche du Temps Perdu*), added some features of similar places he had known when in the army and made it Doncières, a grey, misty, place where it is always autumn and where an essential mystery and melancholy (which Thérèse also recalled) transmute the pale globes of gilded gas lamps, and even bugle-notes and grinding tram wheels, into a haunting melody.[11]

Present-day Lisieux is a shadow of its former self. In Thérèse's lifetime it contained many picturesque fifteenth- and sixteenth-century wooden houses, some of which were decorated with grotesque carvings, but most of its dwellings were dangerously inflammable and the Martins were saved by the fire brigade on at least one occasion. The inadequate housing was noted in a contemporary survey of France by Jules Verne, who had no praise for the town but only for its 'beautiful' and 'attractive' environs.[12] The textile industry was already in decline and unemployment, bankruptcy, alcoholism, sickness, crime and the suicide and mortality rate were on the increase. A large part of the population was anticlerical, even violently so, as was the local republican newspaper, *Le Lexovien*. Thérèse's father belonged to a Catholic social organization set up to combat this tendency, and her uncle, Isidore Guérin, monarchist, anti-Semite, anti-trade-unionist and anti-Freemason, was an outspoken religious and political campaigner who supported the rival right-wing paper, *Le Normand*.

In tranquil Les Buissonnets, on the northern edge of the town, Thérèse was protected from the harsh aspects of life in Lisieux. She was cosseted by her sisters. Pauline, now her surrogate mother, was there when she awoke and they said prayers together. The family, entering the cathedral by the Door of Paradise (*la Porte du Paradis*), heard Mass daily. Afterwards Marie gave Thérèse reading lessons. In the afternoon she would walk with her father or sit on the river-bank, observing nature and 'dreaming of heaven' while he fished in the Touques and she looked at the 'grass and the great tall daisies, taller than I ... sparkling with liquid jewels'.[13] Occasionally, after homework, she played in the garden, making coloured mixtures with seeds and bark, or 'herb teas' for her father, who pretended to drink them. Of course she was 'fond of flowers, and in a recess which by some good fortune happened to be in the garden wall, I used to make little altars and decorate them'.[14] In the evening they played draughts or a similar game, or Thérèse sat on her father's knee while Marie read aloud from an instructive book such as Dom Guéranger's *Liturgical Year*. Later Louis sang a soothing song or ballad, or recited favourite verses, before evening prayers were said and Pauline put Thérèse to bed.

Love, family and nature are the main themes of the fifty-five stanzas of 'The Canticle of Céline', the poem in which Thérèse evoked her childhood memories for Céline's twenty-sixth birthday on 28 April 1895. The first thirty-one stanzas cover life in Alençon and at Les Buissonnets and the time Céline devoted to their father, whereas the second half deals with life in Carmel, the rediscovery of natural beauty in Jesus, and the evidence of his love on earth pointing the way to its fullness in heaven:

> I loved the swallows' graceful flight,
> The turtle-doves' low chant at night,
> The lively sound of insects shining bright,
> The grassy valley where they throng
> In song.
>
> . . .
>
> I loved to see glow-worms glisten;
> Near to God the stars in heaven,
> Most of all to see the moon enliven
> The sky by shining silver bright,
> At night.
>
> . . .

The grass is withered in its bed;
The flowers within my hands are dead.
Weary now, heaven's fields I long to tread,
Dear Jesus, and be made anew
With you.

. . .

In you I have the springs, the rills,
The mignonette, the daffodils,
The eglantine, the harebell on the hills,
The trembling poplar, sighing low
And slow.

. . .

The lake and all that valley fair
And, caressed only by the air,
The ocean touched with silver everywhere;
In you their treasures all combined,
I find.[15]

In June 1878 Thérèse's aunt, Madame Guérin, wrote to
Pauline to say that she received regular supplies of straw-
berries from the Martins' kitchen garden; that the geraniums
were coming along well; and that when she went there to pick
two bouquets of roses Thérèse presented her with her own
tiny offering of 'thlapsi' (rock-alyssum). A year later Pauline
remarked to her aunt that 'this baby loves flowers so much',
and that Thérèse was planning to gather vast bunches of lilies
of the valley from the Jardin de l'Etoile.[16] A few years later
Madame Guérin wrote to tell her husband that:

Yesterday, she and Marie came home all decked out in little
bouquets. Marie had cornflowers, Thérèse had forget-me-nots.
All was perfectly arranged. They were wearing their Breton

aprons, with well-made bouquets at each of the corners, on their heads, at the end of their pigtails, and even on their shoes. One was Rosette, the other Bluette.[17]

Nurturing: 3 October 1881–November 1886

When she was eight Thérèse began her unhappy career as a pupil at the Abbey of Our Lady of the Meadows, the Benedictine school in Lisieux. In February or March 1886 she was withdrawn from the school. In 1882 Pauline left the family home to become a nun at the Carmelite Convent in Lisieux. The sensitive Thérèse felt deserted yet again. She began to suffer from strange headaches and an illness that lasted for almost a year and was not resolved until 13 May 1883, when Thérèse experienced 'Our Lady's smile' as a confirmation of her release from depression and entry to a new phase of her life. Pauline encouraged Thérèse spiritually from behind the convent grille. She prepared her sister for her first Communion in 1884, and supported her throughout this time of inner turmoil and fragility.

Every day Thérèse walked to school through the garden of the former bishop's palace. Although Céline and her two Guérin cousins were at the same school, she described the five years spent there as the saddest in her life. Once again, she portrayed herself as a flower, though now as one used to putting out its 'frail roots in a soil specially prepared for it; such a flower does not take kindly to a garden which it shares with a variety of others, many of them hardier than itself, and draw, from a common soil, the vitality it needs.'[18]

Thérèse was bright and industrious but unable to mix with the other girls, who had different tastes and ambitions. She spent her free time playing at being a hermit with Céline or reading. Though in a class with much older girls, she was awarded the top marks and won all the prizes, and this caused some jealousy. Marie-Joseph of the Cross remembered that Thérèse was cheerful and talkative in her family or with the Guérins, but found her schoolmates indifferent to her 'habitual outpourings'. Her idea of enjoyment was not 'the noisy games of children of her own age', but 'to pick flowers, or to go away by herself in the garden or in the country "to play the hermit". She loved nature and the singing of the birds.'[19]

Although Thérèse described Pauline's departure as not only a 'day of tears but also [one] of benediction, when our Lord gathered the first of his flowers from our garden',[20] she remembered her anguish at this addition to the loss of Rosalie and then her mother. Life as it really was seemed 'full of suffering and constant partings'.[21] Thereafter her contact with Pauline was mainly by correspondence and conversations through the grille during weekly visits.

Not long after Pauline left home, Thérèse suffered another blow to her self-esteem. She loved to sketch the countryside and, years later, told her three sisters what a terrible sacrifice it had been for her to say nothing when she was ten and her father asked if she would like to take painting lessons, like Céline. Her eldest sister Marie had intervened sharply, objecting that it would be a waste of money since Thérèse had not the same aptitude as Céline: 'When I told her she need have only expressed her wish to do so, she replied: "Yes, but I did not want to refuse God anything" '.[22] The absence of both her father and her sister Céline affected her severely. Pauline was clothed as a nun on 6 April 1883, and Thérèse was unable to speak to her by herself. In addition, she could not prepare for her first Communion like her classmates because she was too young. She had to live at her uncle's house.

These and other experiences propelled Thérèse into a psychological illness that did not finally resolve itself until Christmas 1886. She grew so shy that she was often thought to be incompetent and stupid. Pauline wrote to Thérèse in the family's flower terminology to say how the worries she was causing made her 'such an ugly flower . . . you would be more lovable by showing me some beautiful roses on your face, always so pale. . . . To make up for the bouquet of worries you will have to come and offer me soon a bouquet of roses.'[23]

Thérèse's state of mind extended to her body, the very sight of which troubled her: 'I was not at ease in it; I was ashamed of it.' The doctor prescribed water therapy but she could scarcely endure being undressed for the treatment. Eventually, however, the detailed descriptions of flower insemination and propagation in her prize-book, Chaudé's *Theology of Plants*, put her own observations and deductions into a perspective that helped to cure her excessive self-consciousness. When Pauline realized that Thérèse was aware of the facts of life, she asked her sister how she had discovered all this: 'She replied that, without seeking for it, she had found it out for herself in nature, by watching the flowers and the birds.' Thérèse also reminded her astonished sister that when the angel Gabriel told Mary she would be a mother she already 'knew everything fully', for she asked him: 'How shall this be, seeing I know not a man?' 'It is not the knowledge of things that is evil,' Thérèse assured Pauline, since: 'Everything that God has made is very good and very noble. For those whom God calls to that state, marriage is a beautiful thing. It is sin which disfigures and defiles it.'[24]

Flowers and her devotion to Mary also contributed to Thérèse's emergence from childhood depression:

> . . . it was my delight to weave garlands of daisies and forget-me-nots for Our Lady's statue. We were then in the lovely month of May, and the earth was adorned with the flowers of Spring. . . . Only the 'Little Flower' drooped, and seemed to have faded for ever. But close beside her was a radiant Sun, the miraculous statue of the Queen of Heaven . . . and towards that glorious Sun the Flower would often turn.[25]

Deeply upset by his daughter's illness, Louis Martin eventually paid for a novena of Masses at the shrine of Our Lady of Victories in Paris, to obtain a cure for his Little Queen. Thérèse was touched 'to the quick'. This demonstration of his faith and love was another major factor in her 'cure'. Another was her sudden identification of Our Lady as her real 'mother' who would never desert her. 'Like a flower that turns its head towards the sun', she began to turn to the statue of Mary that had been so special to Zélie. Thérèse looked back to 13 May 1883 (Pentecost) as one of her 'Days of Grace', when she detected an 'unspeakably kind, sweet and compassionate' look on Mary's face and realized that Thérèse, this 'faded flower', could by easy stages raise its head again and come back to life:

> What penetrated to the very depths of my soul was her gracious smile. Instantly all my pain vanished . . . big tears fell silently, tears of purest heavenly joy. . . . The Little Flower had come back to life. A bright ray from her glorious Sun had brought warmth and light . . . Our Lady's Flower gathered such strength that five years later she unfolded her petals on the fertile mountain of Carmel.[26]

Pauline clearly came to see the importance of flower imagery for Thérèse, whose conception of herself as a 'flower girl' and in the context of flowers encouraged and, indeed, enacted her recovery and progress. Pauline made even the simple planting of a daisy seem a ceremony for Thérèse and wrote to tell her younger sister about the beautiful flowers of the moment in Carmel: 'shepherd's purse, primroses, daisies, gillyflowers, and my dear little flower, the forget-me-not . . . showing me its blue eye and . . . saying: "Think of your dear child with the blue eyes, who is smiling at you from afar" '. When she offered Our Lady a bouquet from Thérèse, Pauline reported, Mary seemed 'all radiant with her little daughter's flowers', so she said a big thank you to Mary 'as tender as it was big, and I begged her to continue her work and to complete it soon'.[27]

In her letters preparing Thérèse for her first Communion, Pauline skilfully switched from real to symbolic flowers by suggesting that Thérèse should please the Child Jesus by offering him all the flowers on her path; then they would not only be a perfume in heaven's gardens but form her own crown there one day. She addressed Thérèse as the 'little rosebud of the rose bush of my affections' who, once opened up by the gentle sun of Jesus' love, would become a rose that she, Pauline, would arrange to its best advantage. She told Thérèse that during Lent she should offer the Child Jesus a 'pretty bouquet made up of acts of virtue', especially flowers gathered in the 'very beautiful garden of gentleness'. When Thérèse laid her tribute at the crib, the little arms of the holy Child would 'press the dear bouquet of virtues and the little flower girl also gently to his heart'. Because they would bloom in the garden of prayer her prayers to God and Our Lady would also be very beautiful and magnificently scented. Thérèse would draw profit from everything just as the 'bee gathers honey from the tiniest flowers'. When Thérèse was ill, Pauline assured her 'little white rose' that she was praying to Jesus to take up his brush to colour 'with a heavenly and lasting ruby the pallor of your darling cheeks' and make her a 'truly fresh rose'.[28]

Thérèse used similar imagery in her letters:

> I want to be better and in every hole put a pretty little flower, which I shall offer to the Child Jesus in preparation for my First Communion . . . how happy I shall be when the Child Jesus comes into my heart, to have so many lovely flowers to offer him.[29]

From February to May 1884, as she prepared Thérèse for her first Communion, Pauline's flower imagery became more intense. She developed a spiritual dialogue pointing the 'little rose's' way to Carmel in which Pauline's floral symbolism mingled with Thérèse's own, and became established in her vocabulary and an essential theme in her spirituality. It was a natural progression for Thérèse to dedicate her Manuscript A, in which the flower theme predominates, to her 'little Mother'.

Pauline had already prepared Céline for her first Communion. She now sent Thérèse the fruits of her practice: a copybook covered in blue velvet with the initials 'T. M.' embroidered in white by another nun. It contained ninety-six pages, one for each day, with a decorative border, an illuminated date, the name of a flower and an invocation that fitted the scent of the flower. Each of its four sections was prefaced with prayers.[30] Pauline said that Marie would explain the book and help Thérèse to make her whole garden bloom for the great day when Jesus would 'come to rest in this little child's heart, in my Theresita's heart! . . . sleeping among flowers!' Thérèse found the book entrancing, and the prayers 'sweet-scented like roses'.

> What a beautiful picture in the front! It is a little dove giving its heart to the Child Jesus. That's what I'll do with mine! I intend to adorn it with all the lovely flowers I find, so as to offer it to the Child Jesus on the day of my First Communion. . . . I want the Child Jesus to be so happy in my heart that he won't think of going back to heaven.[31]

At this point she began to conceive of devout thoughts and actions almost as actual flowers, as movements of the heart gradually woven into a sacred tribute within her. She united the image of the Infant Jesus and the first stirrings of maternal instinct in a unique application of her floral imagery. The book, she said, taught her to 'stir up in my heart fresh transports of love and fill it anew with flowers. Every day . . . I made a number of little sacrifices and acts of love . . . to be transformed into so many flowers to form within me a cradle for the Holy Child.'[32]

The cradle was as finely constructed as a spider's web. Over the prescribed period of sixty-eight days, between 1 March and 7 May 1884, Thérèse recorded a total of 1,949 little acts of mortification and virtue under the name of a different flower for each day, although she categorized them all as 'roses', sometimes varying the adjective, so that, for instance, 'white roses' appear on 1 March and 'Christmas roses' on 10 March. The numerical achievement was impressive. By 7 May, for example, by repeating Pauline's suggested invocations, such as 'Little Jesus, I love you' or 'Little Jesus, may I always be simple and docile' 2,773 times, she had obeyed Pauline's injunction to 'plant flowers in this garden which are just as beautiful as those in the little copybook' and not allow 'one single weed in it'.[33]

The interchange of letters between the two sisters strengthened the floral context so that it became not a mere aid to, but an essential part of, preparation for Communion and the construction of Thérèse's religious mentality. On 27 and 28 February 1884, for instance, Thérèse drew a little plot of tiny flowers of many colours at the end of her beige diary and on 28 February Pauline wrote to praise her gardening, but also to urge her to new horticultural efforts, for there was still much work to be done sowing so many flowers in so short a time. Yet, as she reminded her sister, there were already buds on the trees in gardens, and the flowers would soon come out: 'if your little garden is in bloom, if all is ready when the great day arrives, believe that Jesus will not come with empty hands!' Over the next two months she tirelessly reinforced the message. Thérèse should not relax her efforts, for even an instant lost would be a 'flower less in the little garden'. She thanked Thérèse for her 'pretty bouquets' and, since the days were passing so quickly and Jesus was approaching, enjoined her not to 'grow tired of your gardening'. She enquired anxiously for assurances that the 'little garden' was on the way to being 'covered over with flowers', asked if Thérèse was aware that flowers needed warmth in order to bloom, insisted that not a single flower should escape, for it would be 'bad to see in your garden a little corner of soil not in bloom', and even reached the ceiling of exaggeration when she assured Thérèse that the 'garden in bloom' she was preparing for Jesus would be 'more delightful than all heaven's gardens!' She comforted her younger sister with the thought that Jesus would enter not only Thérèse's but Pauline's 'poor garden' at the same time, and conveyed an important message:

> I am Theresita's Jesus; I have just left heaven to visit the little flower garden she has been preparing for Me for three months. . . . I will never leave the pretty lily cradle where I'm going to sleep . . . as long as the lilies don't fade![34]

Thérèse described the day of her first Communion, 8 May 1884, as 'the most beautiful day of all the days of my life'. For her the communicants' white dresses were 'snowflakes' and she compared the actual moment of Communion to an indescribably precious and evanescent distillation of all her flowers:

> Some things lose their fragrance when exposed to air, and one's innermost thoughts cannot be translated into earthly words without instantly losing their deep and heavenly meaning. . . . How sweet was the first embrace of Jesus! It was indeed an embrace of love. I felt that I was loved, and I said: 'I love you, and I give myself to you for ever.'[35]

★　★　★

Thérèse used and was influenced by visual as well as verbal floral images. At that time holy pictures (small cards bearing often somewhat debased versions of works by great masters, or sometimes a clipped photographic reproduction in a framework of drawn or hand-painted flowers or symbols) were a kind of visual currency among Catholics. Members of her family sent holy pictures to each other on feast-days and special occasions such as a first Communion. Pauline sent Thérèse an image of the 'Little Flower of the Divine Prisoner' in preparation for her first Communion and Thérèse depicted herself as the 'Little White Flower' on the right-hand side of her 'Coat-of-Arms' at the end of Manuscript A. She relied on her own immediate impressions when sketching the country-side while holidaying with her Guérin cousins, but, when asked to produce drawings and paintings in the convent, she based these works on images she found in holy pictures, as if she now felt that humility required her to be derivative. Since she had had no drawing lessons apart from those offered by Céline, and Céline 'improved' many of Thérèse's images after her sister's death, it would be unfair to make any critical judgement of Thérèse's artwork. Visual imagery was certainly important to her:

> . . . dearest Mother, I owe some of the best and strongest impressions which have encouraged me in the practice of all that is good, to the beautiful pictures you used to show me. While I looked at them, the hours passed unheeded. The 'Little Flower of the Divine Prisoner', for instance, suggested so many thoughts that the sight of it would cast me into a kind of ecstasy. . . . I would offer myself to our Lord to be his little flower.[36]

In Pauline's old painting-room she created her private visual world as a stimulus to meditation and reverie, which could last for hours. She herself compared it to the jumble of a bazaar. She treated it like a collage-artist. Among many other things it included an ink-stand and favourite drawings, a basket of grasses and flowers, a statue of Our Lady, not one caged bird but an aviary, vases always filled with fresh flowers, candles, statues of various saints, shell-work baskets, and a garden suspended in front of the window where she cultivated pots of flowers ('the rarest I could find'), and inside this little 'museum' within the bazaar, a flower-stand on which she placed her privileged plant.[37] Accordingly, she decorated as a temple garden an enclosure inside the house which was itself within a garden; and inside that constructed an intermediate garden containing yet another space for living flowers. She herself, both flower and gardener, moved from one garden sphere to another, tending the plots and plants that were emblems of her own soul. That, too, was another enclosure within the Little Flower, where yet another space – a cradle for Jesus – was actually being plaited entirely from flowers.

The sisters constantly portrayed themselves as flowers. For Pauline, Thérèse and Céline were her 'Lily immortelle' and 'Little Lily', her 'two dear flowers' whose perfume was not 'wasted on earth', but kept for the heavenly meadow of verdure towards which they were 'flying'. They were 'my flowers' which she loved 'only for the sake of Jesus'.[38] She described her meditation on a cherry as the beautiful fruit that had replaced a flower now reduced to a discoloured residue. The youthful love and desire of all three sisters, she wrote, would become like the 'little red fruit in the gentle sun of the Heart of Jesus', and asked them to pray that her own flower would soon dry out and the cherry be good to pick.[39]

Unfurling: December 1886–8 April 1888

Thérèse experienced Christmas Day 1886 as another 'Day of Grace of Conversion' on which the 'third stage of her life' had begun. Her resolve to enter Carmel became all the stronger. She vanquished her excessive shyness and went on to discover her mission to save sinners, which she was sure would continue after her death but had already started with the 'conversion' of her first delinquent, the convicted murderer Pranzini, the moment before his execution on 31 August. Thérèse had prayed fervently for his conversion. When she read an account of the execution in the Catholic paper, *La Croix* (1 September 1887), she interpreted Pranzini's last-minute request to kiss the crucifix as God's sign that her prayers had been answered. She called Pranzini her 'first child'.[40]

She also began to pay more attention to people outside her home environment and taught the catechism to two little girls whose mother (the maid's relative) had died, and whom the Martins had taken into the house when the mother was ill. She gave them each a medal of Our Lady and compared herself to a gardener whom God allowed to 'cultivate rare and delicate plants, providing him with the necessary skill to accomplish it, while reserving to himself the task of making them grow', extending her simile with a reference to grafting: 'What would happen if an ignorant gardener did not properly graft his trees? What if he endeavoured, without understanding the nature of each, to grow roses on peach trees?'[41]

Thérèse chose the feast of Pentecost on 29 May 1887 to tell her father that she had decided to enter Carmel. Later she recalled not his exact words but his symbolic action when he showed her:

> some little white flowers, like miniature lilies, which were growing on a low wall. Picking one, he gave it to me, and remarked with what loving care God had brought it to bloom and preserved it until that day.
>
> I thought I was listening to my own life story, so close was the resemblance between the little flower and little Thérèse. I

received it as a relic, and I noticed that in trying to pluck the slender blossom, Papa had pulled it up by the roots . . . it seemed destined to live on, but in other and more fertile soil. . . . He had just done the same thing for me, by permitting me to leave the sweet valley of my childhood's years for the mountain of Carmel.[42]

She fastened the little white flower to a picture of Our Lady of Victories, so that the Infant Jesus seemed to hold it in his hand, and placed it in her copy of the *Imitation of Christ*, where it remained for years, although the stalk was 'now broken close to the root. No doubt God wishes me to understand by this that he will soon sever all the earthly ties of his Little Flower, and will not leave her to fade here below.'[43]

If Louis Martin was ready to agree to Thérèse's wishes, her uncle was not. On 8 October 1887, Thérèse asked his permission to enter Carmel at Christmas. He replied, '. . . only the world, I fancy, is an obstacle. It would be a real *public scandal* to see a *child* entering Carmel.'[44] Nevertheless, writing to M. Guérin in the language of flowers in which Thérèse's life was now so passionately conceived and experienced by both sisters, Pauline explained why Thérèse wanted to enter the convent, and was able to persuade him to agree to the move. She compared Thérèse to a 'lily-bud opened before the dawn'. Her uncle, she wrote, should let God do what he would do, since at the present moment she feared 'more than ever to hold back this hand lowered with love on our lily in flower!'[45] When Thérèse visited him the next day, M. Guérin had duly changed his mind and, adopting Pauline's metaphor, announced his decision in the same context of flowers: 'I scarcely knew my uncle, so sympathetic had he become.' He no longer made any mention of 'human prudence', but 'told me that I was a little flower that God wanted to pluck, and he himself would no longer oppose it!'[46]

On 4 November 1887 their father took Thérèse and Céline on a pilgrimage to Rome to present a petition to the Pope about Thérèse's early entry to Carmel. Thérèse was impressed by the beauties of nature she saw as they passed through Switzerland. In dutiful imitation of Lamartine and Chateaubriand she celebrated them as evidence of the grandeur of God, yet typically included her own particular observation of plants among the borrowed phraseology. She praised the country's 'lofty mountains, whose snowy peaks are lost in the clouds, its rushing torrents . . . its deep valleys with their luxuriant growths of giant ferns and purple heather . . . poetry and grandeur, a foretaste of the wonders of Heaven . . . a glimpse of what is reserved for those who love Him'.[47]

In the Campo Santo cemetery in Milan she singled out a sculpted child with whom she could identify, for it was throwing flowers on its parents' grave: 'as the delicate petals seem to fall through its fingers, the solid nature of the marble is forgotten'.[48] In Rome she discovered the affinity with the rose-crowned St Cecilia that she would never forget and took up some earth from the supposed site of her patron's tomb. She made her personal appeal to the Pope for permission to enter the convent although she was only fifteen. He did not grant it and, despite his finally encouraging 'Well, child! well, you will enter if it be God's will!', she left Rome in a typically mixed mood of 'peace only in the depths but a troubled exterior'. Returning to France, she passed through stretches of fields covered with orange trees with ripe fruit on them, green olive trees with delicate leaves, and feathery palms. As night fell, the 'stars crept out and shone tremulously in the dark blue sky', but 'it was without regret that I watched this fairy picture fade from my eyes, for my heart was set elsewhere'.[49] Now she was to experience yet another period of 'tribulations' before the 'Little Flower was translated to the mountain of Carmel'; Jesus' 'tears and blood became her dew',[50] and she could look forward to 'greater wonders' than the beauties of nature.

★ ★ ★

Childhood is the paradise in many nineteenth-century writers' works, which were composed at a time when incurable disease, the inescapable hazards of childbirth, and the cruelties and misadventures of the world of work constantly menaced young adults. As in Thérèse's case, tuberculosis alone cut short many lives of great creative promise. In the midst of pain and suffering, childhood was often a period to look back to for images of undoubted bliss and genuine affection. As late as 1896–7, towards the end of her life, when expressing her ardent love for Jesus, Thérèse still resorted to her memory of strewing flowers as a little girl at Les Buissonnets.[51]

Thérèse's infancy afforded intimations of immortality as she struck her 'tender roots deeper and deeper into the dearly loved garden of home' and its surroundings of flowerbeds, park and Norman countryside. There she was protected from the poverty, anticlericalism, irreligion and urban gloom of Lisieux outside her domain, but also the 'marble staircases, gilded ceilings and silken hangings' of the more privileged, artificial world she knew only from the grand hotels of her Italian journey and, to a lesser degree, from visits to relatives. Together with personal experiences of unhappiness, these traces of a world that she rejected remained as minor discordant notes in her imaginative and spiritual melody. But she did not reject the delights of nature and the affections of home life. These she 'sacrificed', which meant that they were among the major themes and notes, the flowers actual and metaphorical, which Thérèse's ardent mind and spirit (her 'âme en fleur') carried from her childhood into the enclosed garden of Carmel and developed there as a uniquely resonant composition.

❧ 3 ❧

1888–1897

The sounds of passionate impulse within a solitary heart are like the murmuring of winds and waters in the silence of a desert.

François-René de Chateaubriand

Never again shall I see the places of childhood, / The meadows radiant and laughing with flowers . . . / I dream of scents, of the sweet morning dew, / . . . of the magic of woods, valleys and fields.

Thérèse of Lisieux

Blossoming: 9 April 1888–September 1890

The fifteen-year-old Thérèse achieved her immediate earthly goal when she entered the 'desert of Carmel' on 9 April 1888. The Carmel of Lisieux was established in 1838 in descent from the original foundation of the thirteenth-century hermits who retreated to the wooded outcrop of Mount Carmel, overlooking Haifa in Palestine, to live a prayer-based community life in the spirit of the prophet Elijah. Thérèse entered as a postulant. The postulantship represented the status of application for full entry, was largely devoted to prayer, and usually lasted six months to a year before clothing. Thérèse's clothing ceremony, during which she exchanged secular for religious dress and wore a crown of roses for the day to symbolize her marriage to Christ, was on 10 January of the following year. She thus entered the novitiate (usually lasting one to two years). This period ended on 8 September 1890 with her profession, when she took vows of poverty, chastity, and obedience (sometimes a fourth vow is added, such as caring for the sick, activity for the poor, or working on foreign missions), and once again wore a crown of roses. Having taken this definitive step, she felt profoundly happy and peaceful.

The Lisieux Carmel was a red-brick building close to the Orbec (or Orbiquet) river. Although she now saw herself as a 'hidden flower which keeps its perfume only for Heaven', and her acquaintance with the natural world outside was supplied from memory, prayer, liturgy and reading, so that the actual merged ever more with the symbolic in her consciousness, she was not wholly cut off from nature. She was exposed to sunlight and saw plants and their setting either through the cloisters, which gave on to a courtyard with twenty rose bushes, or through the triangular garden beyond the east wing. There a walk planted with chestnut trees skirted a little hayfield, or 'meadow', where pear trees grew.

She said later that she found 'everything in the convent delightful',[1] especially her cell, which was about ten feet by seven, had simple whitewashed or plastered walls, no running water, no heating of any kind, and no electric light, and contained only a bed and a basic bookshelf. Although afternoon sunlight reached Thérèse through the window, there was no view.

In spite of her inner calm she did not find convent life easy and in her autobiography admitted that she experienced spiritual difficulties and was racked by scruples about sinning inadvertently by finding herself in the wrong frame of mind for a nun: 'Yet you know well, dear Mother, that from the very outset my path was strewn with thorns rather than roses!'[2]

Mother Marie de Gonzague, the prioress, was difficult and eccentric, inclined to sudden changes of mood and fancy, and the adoption of favourites. She had been an enthusiastic supporter of Thérèse's admission at an atypically young age, yet treated her severely and constantly humiliated her. The nuns suffered from the prioress's unstable rule, which could be countered only by subtle anticipation and diplomatic manoeuvres. Inevitably some of them copied her attitude by scolding the new entrant and by giving her leftovers or old herring-heads to eat, and similar acts of spite masquerading as training in humility. Thérèse accepted this treatment as suffering for God and assured Céline that she was happy and was adequately fed.

For a time Thérèse had a reassuring spiritual guide in the person of Father Pichon, Marie's spiritual Director. Thérèse corresponded with him when he was sent to Canada as a missionary but felt the loss, decided to turn to Jesus himself, the 'Director of directors', and began 'gradually to unfold' in the personal relationship with God that was the essence of her spirituality.

This did not exclude but relied on certain devotional metaphors and practices that fitted her self-image as a 'little flower' and the 'busy cultivation of the garden of her heart' as a resting-place for the Child Jesus, which Pauline had recommended when preparing Thérèse for her first Communion. On entering Carmel she became 'Thérèse of the Child Jesus'. Although many people nowadays will find this rather odd, there were various devotions to the Holy Infant in nineteenth-century France, particularly among the Carmelites.

The statue of the Infant Jesus of Prague, known as '*Divin Petit Grand*', holding a globe in his left hand as a symbol of Christ's dominion over the world in the sense that 'in him all things hold together' (Col. 1: 17), stood on the novitiate altar of the Lisieux Carmel. To some it was a spur to sentimental piety; to others an image of the truth expressed by St Bernard of Clairvaux in the words: 'The greatest of all beings has become the least of all and accomplished this wonder, Love.'[3] For Thérèse the profound meaning of the pun was clear, for '*le plus petit*' was both 'the least of all' and 'the littlest', and she had several copies of a holy picture bearing paraphrases of St Bernard's text.

The statue of the Child Jesus of Beaune stood at the end of the tribune near the choir. The cult of the Infant of Beaune had originated after 1630, when Marguerite Parigot, eleven-and-a-half years old, entered the Carmel of Beaune after her mother's death. She learned the veneration of the Holy Child from the Spanish nuns there and claimed that he appeared to her, helped her with her work, taught her how he should be honoured from his birth to his twelfth year, and eventually required veneration as King of Kings, so that he was portrayed with crown and sceptre. Supported by an influential patron, and accompanied by miracles of healing, the cult spread in France. Thérèse liked to decorate the statue of the Beaune Infant with flowers, as she did that of the Child Jesus in the cloister. She was soon put in charge of the little grotto-shrine of the Child Jesus, which she had painted in rose-pink and made sure was always surrounded with brightly-coloured wild flowers and tiny, prettily-feathered stuffed birds.

As a postulant, Thérèse was prescribed light weeding in the garden at half past four every evening before prayers, for the sake of fresh air, so she had some contact with growing things. Nevertheless, she was beginning to regret the relative absence of the field and meadow flowers she had loved so much, when the portress carried in a sheaf of wheat and wild flowers which someone had left on the window ledge of the 'extern sister', facing the 'secular world' outside. Thérèse was allowed to take them to her Holy Child shrine. This started a tradition of ensuring that the Carmel had a regular supply of flowers of the field, which Thérèse recorded as an important aspect of her life there: 'I gave up for ever the delight of rambling through meadows bright with the treasures of spring. . . . Yet I received . . . an abundance of all the flowers I loved best: cornflowers, poppies, marguerites.' She particularly missed the little purple vetch which she had picked in the country-side around Alençon, but when this too arrived to 'make me smile', she interpreted it as a special favour in return for her sacrifice.[4] She liked to arrange sweet-smelling flowers in a large basket by the Holy Child statue, but had to replace them with artificial flowers as Mother Hermance of the Heart of Jesus, a cantankerous elderly nun, could not tolerate even the scent of a violet. One day, when she was about to place a wax rose in front of the statue, Mother Hermance called out to complain. Thérèse was strongly tempted to let her do so, but decided to sacrifice the pleasure, held out the flower and exclaimed happily: 'Look, Mother, how well they imitate nature nowadays! Wouldn't you think that this rose had just been freshly gathered from the garden?'[5]

While Thérèse was in Carmel, Pauline and Marie con-tinued to encourage her view of flowers as symbols of sacri-fice. When on a retreat before her profession, Marie sent Thérèse a letter enclosing a violet. Thérèse replied that the letter had filled her 'with fragrance'. She had had the little violet dried carefully and asked Marie to pray that Thérèse would remain 'very obscure, hidden from all eyes, that Jesus alone' might be able to see her. She wished to 'become smaller and smaller' and to be 'reduced to a nothing'.[6] Marie also sent her a memento of her retreat inscribed on the verso with a typical invocation to the Cherubim in which the tra-ditional language of bridal mysticism became emphatically floral. They were asked to lead the devout reader into the Bridegroom's garden: 'Will I be the little plant upon whom he is going to look with pleasure and whose flower he will pick in order to breathe in its scent? . . . Open your petals and

bend the flower of your heart towards him.'[7] On 22 May
Thérèse, the youngest sister, crowned her eldest sister with
roses on the day of her mystical marriage.

On 7 June 1888, the eve of the feast of the Sacred Heart,
Pauline wrote to Marie (Sister Marie of the Sacred Heart) as
the 'poor little rose of Jesus' and on behalf of Thérèse, the
'dear bud', to offer the 'blessed Rose of the Heart of Jesus' all
their good wishes, and it seems, enclosed three roses and a
bud, which Marie, as she wrote to tell their father, placed
before the statue of Jesus.[8]

Thérèse and her sisters also used floral language to express,
discuss and console for 'sadness' and 'aridity' and the 'pinpricks' of community life, as revealed, for instance, in the fourteen notes Thérèse exchanged with those close to her during
the retreat before her clothing ceremony on 10 January 1889.
Sister Marie of the Angels (her novice-mistress) reminded her
that some little flowers needed more shade than sun to
develop fully, and that sadness of spirit might be the treatment
the divine Gardener had decided was best for her soul.[9] When
Thérèse wrote to Pauline to say she was in 'darkness', her
sister raised their common language to a new intensity, which
might now seem rather heady and inappropriately erotic but
was wholly in line with the bridal language of the Song of
Songs (which she cited) and of medieval and baroque mysticism. She assumed the persona of the Gardener addressing
Thérèse's soul as the 'Dear garden of my little fiancée', and
asked her to remain an enclosed garden open only to him: 'I
am the sun of your flowers. My divine eyes will cast such a ray
of flame upon your budding fruits that they will ripen in one
instant . . . my friend, my sister, my dove, open to me.'[10]

Thérèse began to translate other natural phenomena and
especially those connected with propitious events into the
predominantly floral language of her system of correspondences, which was simultaneously familial and divine. Even

snowflakes were converted appropriately. On 10 January 1889, after receiving the habit and embracing her father for the last time, Thérèse retired from the area outside the cloister to the enclosed part of the convent. She turned from the Holy Child smiling at her among flowers and lights to find the quadrangle covered, miraculously it seemed, for the day was warm, by a sudden fall of snow sent by 'him who loves lilies white as the snow'.[11]

She had added 'of the Holy Face' to her name in religion, as Pauline had advised her before the statue of the Child Jesus of the Carmel of Beaune. On 26 April 1885, her father, Léonie, Céline and Thérèse had joined the confraternity of the Holy Face, based on the cult promoted by a Monsieur Dupont (1797–1876) in obedience to the revelations of the Carmelite Sister Marie of Saint Peter (1816–1848) and highly favoured by Mother Geneviève of Saint Teresa, the foundress of the Carmel at Lisieux. However disparate they now seem in an age no longer used to thinking in terms of associations that unite natural and supernatural in a coherent scheme, for nineteenth-century Catholics the Child Jesus and the Holy Face were closely connected. Images of the Child Jesus showed him contemplating his future passion, or holding a cross or crown of thorns in his hand. Sometimes his manger was shaped like a cross. In the French devotional and mystical tradition derived from Bérulle, who became Superior of the Paris Carmel, Jesus' entire life expressed his continual acceptance of his Father's mission. Although the main aim of the Holy Face cult was to make reparation for insults and blasphemies committed in the name of Jesus, Thérèse, the first Carmelite in Lisieux to add 'of the Holy Face' to her name, saw the devotion more as a means of contemplating Jesus' love, as an aid to the religion of the heart. Like the Veronica who is said to have wiped Jesus' face during the Passion and to have received its impression on cloth (or veil) and soul, Thérèse (instructed by Pauline) saw herself as the 'little Veronica', both within and in herself an enclosed garden where she could console Jesus. There, too, she could be imprinted with his face, as she asked in the prayer 'Make me like you, Jesus' which she kept in a little container pinned to her chest. For Thérèse, the image of the Holy Face on processional banners used for occasions of communal worship became the emblem of an intimate relationship with the Divine. She began to see herself not only as the smiling flower but also as the 'veil of the smile'. She was not merely hidden in Carmel but sought obscurity in the deeper sense of a desire to be misunderstood and thus imitate the 'Face that was not recognized even by your own disciples!'[12]

She also associated the Holy Face with gardens because her father had created an arbour known as the Hermitage of the Holy Face in the garden at Les Buissonnets. It was presented to the Carmel and placed near the chestnut-tree walk, when, on 12 February 1889, he was committed to a private asylum in Caen. Thérèse put her painting of the Holy Face in the arbour, which was now near the alley of chestnut trees. Symbolically, it was now in the garden of her heart, itself enclosed within a garden. She was devastated by her father's illness ('I no longer protested that I could suffer more . . . there are no words to express our grief ').

Pauline painted a miniature version of the Holy Face on parchment and gave it to Céline. Thérèse was deeply moved by this image of the Face bleeding and surrounded by nine lilies on a green stem intertwined with a branch of thorns, and showing Céline as the white lily whose petals supported the Holy Face. The stem was their mother in heaven; their father the branch of thorns chosen by Jesus to be a victim; and the four little buds the Martin children who died in infancy. 'Yes,' Thérèse wrote, 'our family is a *lily-branch*, and the *Lily without name* resides in the midst . . . as a king. . . . His divine blood flows out upon our petals, and his thorns tear us so that the perfume of our love can breathe forth.'[13] Pauline also wrote a prayer to the Holy Face which helped Thérèse to discover the 'hidden beauties of Jesus', for his features were compared to a festal bouquet, with 'night lilies' (*belles-de-nuit*, or four o'clocks) as his eyes, and the 'Flower of Flowers' as Jesus himself.[14] Writing to Pauline, who was making a private annual retreat, Thérèse asked her to tell Jesus to look on her, so 'that the *night lilies* may penetrate with their luminous rays the heart of the grain of sand . . . ask also that the *Flower of flowers* may open its petals and that the melodious sound that comes forth may set its mysterious teachings vibrating in the heart'.[15]

The flower symbolism of the letters Thérèse, once in the convent, wrote to her family, especially those to Céline, reveals her increasing self-knowledge and deepening spirituality but also her desire to maintain the interconnectedness of their thinking at a suitable level. The strain shows when she begins to analyse the family relationship, then almost to preach and assume the instructional role formerly practised by her sisters. In one letter she refers to the *Lis-immortelle*, the flower symbol assigned to Céline by Pauline, using the feminine of 'immortel' (immortal) without agreement with the masculine *lis* (lily):

> There is something so sensitive between our souls that makes them so much alike. We have always been together, our joys, our pains, everything has been in common. . . . I feel that this is continuing in Carmel . . . only the yellow lily [the Martins' term for marriage] could separate us a little. I tell you this because I am sure that the white lily will always be your lot since you have chosen him and he has chosen you first. . . . You know that your soul is a lily immortelle. Jesus can do all he wills with it. It matters little whether it be in one place or another; it will always be immortelle. The tempest cannot make the yellow of its stamen

fall on its white scented calyx; it is Jesus who made it that way.
. . . At the side of this Lily, Jesus has placed another, its faithful
companion. . . . One was weak, the other was strong; Jesus took
the weak one, and he left the other so as to embellish it with a
new splendour. . . . Jesus asks ALL from His two lilies; he wills to
leave them nothing but their white dress. ALL! Has immortelle
understood her sister? . . .

Each new suffering, each heart's pain, is a gentle wind to bear
to Jesus the fragrance of his lily; then he smiles lovingly, and
immediately makes ready a new grief . . . the more his lily grows
in love, the more it must grow in suffering too. . . . We are greater
than the whole universe. One day we shall have, even we, a divine
existence. . . . I thank Jesus for thus giving a lily to be with our
dearest Father, a lily which nothing affrights, a lily which would
die rather than desert the *glorious* field in which Jesus' love has
placed it![16]

Sometimes Thérèse's flower metaphors were assuring repe-
titions of a family convention, as when she asked for warm
thanks to be given to 'my darling little Marie for her enchant-
ing bouquet, tell her that I am giving it to Jesus from her, and
that I am asking him in return to adorn her soul with as many
virtues as there are rosebuds!'[17] But their purpose and expression could be more complex, as when Thérèse's anxiety to
ensure Céline's spiritual welfare and protect her from 'the
world' merged with sisterly concern for her. Then floral and
natural imagery provided the context in which the two
interests could appear as one and the same, as when she
wrote to Céline on tour with her family:

. . . you must be very happy to contemplate nature in her beauty,
the mountains, the silvery streams, all so magnificent, so calcu-
lated to raise up our souls . . . little Sister, let us detach ourselves
from the earth and fly up to the mountain of Love where grows

the lovely Lily of our souls. Let us detach ourselves from Jesus' *consolations*, to attach ourselves to *Him* . . . the Face of the loveliest and whitest of Lilies . . .

Céline, pure hearts are often ringed with thorns, often in darkness, then the lilies think they have lost their whiteness, think that the thorns which ring them round have actually torn their petals. . . . The lilies in the midst of thorns are those whom Jesus loves, it is in their midst that he takes his pleasure![18]

Thérèse's spiritual progress entered a new phase with her profession: 'Next morning, 8 September, my soul was flooded with heavenly joy, in that peace "which surpasseth understanding" I pronounced my holy vows . . .' and, at the close of that 'glorious day I laid my crown of roses . . . at our Lady's feet . . . it was without regret; I felt that time could never take away my happiness'. Yet, the evening before, she had seen 'darkness everywhere' as she was seized with doubts about her vocation, dispelled only by the novice-mistress's kindness and Reverend Mother's laughter. On 24 September 1890 she was veiled. Her father was in a mental home, Father Pichon in Canada, and the Bishop too ill to attend, so the dark mood returned 'in a mist of tears' and the calyx of the little flower was filled with 'sadness and bitterness' (*tristesse et amertume*), yet 'there was peace deep down in my cup'.[19]

Propagating: October 1890–March 1896

Thérèse continued to throw flowers to commemorate special occasions. One occurred not long after she took the veil. She had prayed to St Joseph for more frequent Communion, for daily Communion was a rare privilege in convents at that time, and she suffered from this privation. A decree of Pope Leo XIII of 17 December 1890 allowed confessors of religious houses to permit more frequent reception, and thereafter Thérèse, finding her petition answered, scattered flowers before St Joseph's statue whenever she passed it, even though Abbé Youf, the somewhat recalcitrant confessor of Carmel, allowed her to receive Communion daily only during the influenza epidemic of December 1891–January 1892.

Thérèse's personal concerns had a communal dimension and she told the Sisters that she was sure that daily Communion would soon be introduced as a norm in the convent (as happened after her death). Her feelings of compassion had long been focused on her desire to be a missionary, a possibility she still entertained ('Will the Little White Flower be gathered in all her freshness, or will she be transplanted to other shores?'[20]). She was asked to assist other nuns, and her hitherto obsessive concern with her own spiritual development became more mature and profound as she concentrated on helping others through their trials and disappointments as part of an ambitious vision of bringing humanity closer to God. She started with her sister, Céline, writing her a series of quasi-poetical letters, and continued with her sisters in religion and 'spiritual brothers'. She might be said to have devised and honed her 'Little Way' so that they could follow her own example. Inevitably, the conviction and power of her language were major factors in this process. When the subprioress, Sister Marie of the Angels, sent a description of Thérèse to the Visitation Convent of Mans she said not only that she was tall and strong, with a childlike appearance, yet always in harmony and self-possessed in everything and with everybody, but emphasized her possession of a 'tone of voice and way with words that gives her wisdom and clarity of mind beyond her years', and her ability, whether in mystical or comical mode, to 'make you weep with devotion or collapse with laughter'.[21]

Thérèse was an imaginative and original teacher. Céline recalled that she asked Thérèse for help when she felt discouraged and was unable to rise above her trial. 'This does not surprise me', she replied, 'for we are too small to rise above our difficulties. Therefore let us try to pass under them.'[22]

Thérèse also wrote to Céline using flower symbolism in the same mode that Pauline had used in her letters to Thérèse. Thérèse did not want Céline to marry, both because her sister's heart was not physically sound and at one time she had been thought to be in danger of dying prematurely, and because she wanted to encourage her to become Christ's bride and thus 'save' her from the world: 'let us make our heart a little garden of delight where Jesus may come to find rest. . . . Let us plant only lilies in our garden . . . no other flowers, for they can be cultivated by others . . . but only virgins can give Jesus lilies.' She told her that virginity was a 'profound silence of all this world's cares', and that 'everyone has a natural love for the place of his birth, and as the place of Jesus' birth is the Virgin of Virgins and Jesus was born, by his choice, of a Lily, he loves to be in virgin hearts'.[23]

Thérèse saw all her sisters as flowers in a more conventional sense, though still within a devotional context, as she made clear when writing to thank Madame Guérin for sending her presents for her feast day: 'The two pretty pots of flowers given by my two dearest little sisters, Jeanne and Marie . . . are placed in front of the Child Jesus, and at every hour of the day they beg as many graces and blessings [for them] as each bush of heather has tiny flowers.'[24] She transferred them to a meta-physical scheme of reference, however, as she focused intently on Céline's destiny:

> . . . Céline, I am sending you two of your flowers for your feast; you will understand their language. . . . A single stalk bears them, one same sun caused them to grow together, the same ray brought them to blossoming, and surely the same day will see them die! . . . The eyes of creatures do not bother to pause upon

a little *Céline-flower*, yet its white cup is full of mystery. It has in its heart a great number of other flowers, which are of course the children of *its soul* (souls), and then its white calyx is red within, as though stained with its blood! . . . He . . . created it . . . for Himself alone! . . . it is more fortunate than the glowing rose which is not for Jesus alone! . . . a ray from his Heart can in one instant bring his flower to blossoming for eternity![25]

When Céline wrote to describe a suitor (Henry Maudelonde, 1864–1937) whom she found it difficult to reject, Thérèse increased the intensity of her floral efforts to ensure that Céline realized the beauty and sublimity of virginity as a bride of Jesus: 'Céline dearest, let us always remain the lilies of Jesus', she insisted, for 'the grace I ask him is that he takes his lilies from this world before the perilous wind of earth has blown the tiniest bit of pollen that might ever so little stain with its yellow the whiteness and the radiance of the lily'.[26]

Thérèse's heightened floral writing was quite conscious. She did not exist in or write out of a mystico-religious dreamworld, as it were. Although she thought of God all through the day, her mind did not 'dwell on him more in my sleep', for, 'as a rule I dream of the woods and flowers, the brooks and the sea. I nearly always meet pretty children, or else chase birds or butterflies such as I have never seen before. But if my dreams are sometimes poetical, they are never mystical.'[27] The images she used, though disparate, were connected not haphazardly but according to her grand design, as when she wrote to wish Céline a happy feast day:

. . . the Céline-flower . . . contrary to the other flowers . . . [has] blossomed one month before the time of its blossoming. . . . Céline, do you understand the language of my dear little flower . . . the flower of my childhood . . . the flower of our memories?!!! . . . Wintry weather, the rigours of winter, instead of retarding it, made it grow and blossom . . . only the bees know the treasures that its mysterious calyx encloses, made up of a multitude of little calyxes, each one as rich as the others . . . the angels . . . like the vigilant bees, know how to gather the honey contained within the mysterious and multiple calyxes that represent souls or rather the children of the virginal little flower . . . when and how will Jesus pluck his little flower? . . . Perhaps the pink colour of its corolla indicates that this will be by means of martyrdom! . . . Perhaps after having asked us love for love, so to speak, Jesus will want to ask us blood for blood, life for life. . . . In the meantime, we must let the bees draw out all the honey from the little calyxes.[28]

By April of the next year Thérèse's constant reading of Scripture had given her flower parables a new strength and evangelistic fervour, as when she sent Céline a daisy for her twenty-third birthday:

This year the Carmel meadow provides me with a symbolic present . . . a slender stalk more beautiful than the rest . . . not one daisy but two distinct ones . . . the double daisy fixing its eyes upon its Divine Sun carries its own unique mission . . . *Where your treasure is, there is your heart.* Our treasure is Jesus and our hearts make but one heart in him . . . Perhaps the petals that the daisy will present to the Divine Spouse in the evening of its life will have turned red.[29]

When she wrote to Céline for her twenty-fourth birthday, Thérèse had probably seen dewdrops sparkling on the tips of blades of grass in the meadow that very morning, during the procession in honour of St Mark in the Carmel garden, and used dew here to symbolize the nature of the devout life hidden in God, with Céline as the drop of dew in the divine Lily-cup. Thérèse had reached a point where she was able to combine the influences of Chaudé the theologico-botanical divine, Arminjon the cosmic prophet, the Old Testament, the Spanish mystics and the French Romantics, in an accomplished personal style:

> What is simpler and purer than a dewdrop? It is not formed by the *clouds*, because dew falls on the flowers when the vault of heaven is filled with stars. Rain is not to be compared with it, for it surpasses the rain in freshness and beauty. Dew exists only by night; the sun, darting its warm rays upon it, distils the lovely pearls sparkling on the tip of the blades of grass in the meadow, and the dew changes into a light vapour. Céline is a drop of dew, not formed by the clouds but come down from the loveliness of heaven, her Homeland. During the *night* of life, it is its mission to be hid in the heart of the *Flower of the fields*; no human eye can find it, only the cup that holds the tiny dewdrop can know its freshness. . . .
>
> Our Beloved has no need of our fine thoughts – it is not intellect or talents that Jesus has come upon earth to seek. He became the Flower of the fields solely to show us how he loves simplicity. *The Lily in the valley* does not aspire to more than a drop of dew. . . . That is why he created one, called Céline! During the night of this life, she is to remain hid from every human eye, but . . . the moment he appears in his glory . . . the divine Luminary, looking upon his dewdrop, will draw it upward to him, and it will ascend like a light vapour and go where it may abide for eternity in the bosom of the glowing furnace of uncreated Love, forever united with him. . . . Jesus . . . wants his dewdrops not even to be aware of themselves . . . only he regards them; and they, not realizing their value, think of themselves below other creatures . . . and that is what the *Lily of the valleys* desires.[30]

The dewdrop and the wild Flower (or Lily) supplied a constant theme in this period of Thérèse's life. The association with death and heaven was encouraged by her reading of St John of the Cross, for whom God's love was so indescribably omnipotent as to absorb a soul more effectively than a fire-storm might devour a morning dewdrop.[31]

Accordingly, when Pauline anxiously asked Thérèse about dying, Thérèse tried to comfort her by saying that God would sip her up like a little drop of dew.[32] Her task of tending the flowers before the statue of the Child Jesus, and her religious name of Thérèse of the Child Jesus and Holy Face probably influenced the picture of the Child Jesus' dream that Thérèse painted in oils for Pauline in January 1894. Céline retouched it in 1927, and it is now in the Visitation Convent at Chartres. Based on a holy picture given to her by Sister Anne of the Sacred Heart, Thérèse's painting shows the infant Jesus asleep but propped up and holding flowers in his right hand and roses in his lap.[33] Thérèse explained that it was:

> your virtues that I meant to represent by the little flowers Jesus is pressing to his heart. The flowers are indeed for Jesus alone . . . yet, in spite of the humility that would like to conceal them, the mysterious fragrance breathing from these flowers gives me here on earth some faint sense of the marvels I shall see one day . . . when I shall be allowed to gaze on the treasures of love you now lavish upon Jesus.[34]

Thérèse's confident use of floral language was encouraged by Father Armand Lemonnier, who preached at the retreats of 1893, 1894 and 1895. He was particularly fond of such expressions as the 'fragrant roses of our unceasing love'. He spoke of the Carmelite nuns as 'little fragrant flowers, whose sweet scent Jesus loves to breathe'. A Carmelite was a 'little flower he will come one day to gather and transport . . . to the delightful thickets where virgins follow the Lamb everywhere'. His sermons are thought to have inspired Thérèse's Christmas play 'The Angels at Jesus' Crib',[35] which was written just before she started work on the first part of her autobiography (Manuscript A), and in which she compares the human soul to a flower. Here she cites flowers fifteen times and mentions the theme of stripping petals from a flower, which she developed in a later poem.

Thérèse wrote her poems and playlets out of obedience and in the given time. She would memorize for later transcription any ideas or verses that came to her while at her duties. Prayer, which expanded the soul in trials as well as joy, united the individual with God, and saved souls, came first. She was anxious, too, to instruct her charges in the due composition of prayers.

Sister Marie-Madeleine, one of Thérèse's charges, was preparing to receive her habit. To help her Thérèse used flower symbolism and the copybook format as Pauline had done for her sister's first Communion in 1884. Marie-Madeleine was to pick 180 flowers (sacrifices) in two weeks. The novice's 'wedding basket' would have only white flowers, ranging from 'white roses' to 'lilies', and set off by a touch of gold in the form of 'tea roses' and 'honeysuckle'. 'Mystical flowers' for the 'bridal bouquet' appeared on the cover and title page. Aspirations (one for each day, repeated seventeen times) were white roses; daisies represented pleasing Jesus alone; white violets, gentleness and humility; lilies of the valley, saving souls; white roses, serving the community as serving Jesus; tea roses, the grace to make a good retreat; white bellflowers, life as an act of love; honeysuckle, self-denial; white periwinkles, love of God; white peonies, the redemption of sinners; jasmine, joy in Jesus alone; white forget-me-nots, angelic protection; meadowsweet, purity; white verbena, faith and love of God; white iris, thankfulness; and lilies, union with Jesus.[36]

Floral language was an important structuring principle for Thérèse, but flowers were also significant because they were recurrent signs pointing to a divine order that guaranteed the stability missing from her early life. Though they died they would be reborn while remaining rooted in the same ground. Thérèse thought of herself as a springtime flower, a living sign of regeneration promised to the weak and seemingly ephemeral who were strong through trust in God's love. Her 'Little Way' of self-acceptance was based on the gospel. It considered the lilies of the field as they were, and did not seek to assuage but to make sense of depression and anxiety as well as joy.

In January 1895 Thérèse began to write the 'springtime story of a little white flower', dedicated to the Reverend Mother Agnes of Jesus (her sister Pauline), and the summation of her self-image as a flower and of her conception of flowers and the natural creation, of 'marvels so entrancing beneath our feet', as signs and glimpses of the hidden mysteries worked in human souls.

Scattering and Gathering: April 1896–30 September 1897

When she became the auxiliary novice-mistress, the advice Thérèse offered her postulants was similar to the guidance she had received from Pauline when she was preparing for her first Communion. On the day of Sister Marie of the Trinity's profession, Thérèse covered the young nun's bed with forget-me-nots and placed a note on it:

> My dearest little Sister, I should like to have flowers that will not die to give you in memory of this beautiful day, but it is only in heaven that flowers never fade . . . at least these forget-me-nots will tell you that, in your little sister's heart, the memory will always remain deeply graven of the day on which Jesus gave you

the kiss of the *union* which must be completed, or rather, realized in heaven.[37]

For Thérèse the placing, throwing and scattering of flowers was a deeply meaningful act of devotion, blessing or consecration. Real flowers are rarely thrown at a married couple nowadays. They are replaced by the paper confetti originally made from flower petals. Occasionally, however, flowers are still thrown over the hearse and coffin at funerals, and petals are scattered before the statue or monstrance during processions to commemorate a saint or, as on Corpus Christi, to honour the Blessed Sacrament. As a child, Thérèse scattered petals at the feet of St Domitia, or before the Sacrament. She would throw the flowers as high as possible, and watch with delight as they fell on and over the object of devotion. As she developed her 'Little Way' she began to interpret flower-throwing more symbolically, especially under the influence of her reading of St John of the Cross:

> I, the little one, shall strew flowers, perfuming the divine throne with their fragrance. I shall sing Love's canticle in silvery tones. Thus my . . . life will be spent in your sight, my Beloved! To strew flowers is the only means of proving my love, and these flowers will be each word and look, each little daily sacrifice. I wish to make profit out of the smallest actions and do them all for Love. For Love's sake I wish to suffer and to rejoice: so I shall strew my flowers . . . singing all the while, I shall scatter the petals of every one I see before you. . . . Even if I have to gather my flowers among thorns, I shall sing, and the longer and sharper the thorns, the sweeter my song will be.[38]

In her poem of 1896, 'To Scatter Flowers', she was able to enlarge the imagined action and its setting and thus its personal implications of faith, hope and love. The verse conventions and the extended image of flower-throwing allowed her to relate affection, compassion, giving, sacrifice, reparation, belief, trust, chosen restriction and eventual release into joy more effectively than in the lyrical prose passages of the autobiography:

O Jesus! O my Love! Each eve I come to fling
Before your sacred cross sweet flowers of the year.
By their plucked petals fair my hands so gladly bring
I long to dry your every tear!

To scatter flowers, that means each sacrifice:
My lightest sighs and pains, my heaviest, saddest hours,
My hopes, my joys, my prayers, I will not count the price:
Behold my flowers!

With deep untold delight your beauty fills my soul,
Would I might light this love in hearts of all who live!
For this, my fairest flowers, all things in my control,
How fondly, gladly would I give!

To scatter flowers! Behold my chosen sword
For saving sinners' souls and filling heaven's bowers:
The victory is mine – yes, I disarm you, Lord,
With these my flowers!

The petals in their flight caress your holy face;
They tell you that my heart is yours, and yours alone.
You know well what these leaves are saying in my place,
And smile upon me from your throne.

To scatter flowers! That means to speak of you:
My only pleasure here, where tears fill all the hours.
But soon I shall be free, with angels and with you,
And scatter flowers.[39]

By (approximately 8–17) September 1896, Thérèse had
added the missionary aspect to her injunctions on flower-
throwing to Sister Marie of Saint-Joseph. By now the metaphor had to be expanded to surrealistic dimensions to
accommodate the changes in her spiritual thinking, and it
revealed the immense scope of the devout life and the power
of prayer as Thérèse understood them. As a postulant (she
said) Marie, not Jesus, was now the infant, borne in his arms.
Yet she would become a missionary, 'even a warrior', for her
vocation would be to evangelize not one 'but all missions'.
She would do this by loving, by sleeping, and by throwing
flowers to Jesus when he was asleep. 'Then Jesus will take
these flowers, and, giving them an inestimable value, he will
throw them in his turn; he will have them fly over all shores
and will save souls (with flowers, with the love of the little
child . . .).'[40]

Thérèse's notion of flower-throwing as a missionary
endeavour was far from rhetorical. She believed in acting on
the verses which, at about the same time, she copied from the
chapter of Isaiah on the theme 'thou shalt be like a watered
garden', which she found particularly impressive: 'And if thou
draw out thy soul to the hungry, and satisfy the afflicted soul;
then shall thy light rise in obscurity, and thy darkness be as the
noonday.'[41]

She showed deep affection and concern for Sister Marie of
Saint-Joseph, who was then aged thirty-nine. She had lost her
mother when she was only nine, was subject to violent mood
swings from elation through depression to angry outbursts,
and was shunned by the Sisters. Thérèse did not agree with
this treatment, befriended Marie, shared her linen-room
work, and even watched over her while she slept. Most
important of all, Thérèse devised a form of spiritual
psychotherapy for this 'sick soul' similar to the flower
exercises which her sister had used to help her out of her

own childhood depression. She set her 'child' Marie's emotions and aspirations in a context of universal love and achievement, and duly became the 'restorer of paths to dwell in' of Isaiah 58.

She continued to develop her own self-understanding in the same setting. In November 1896 Thérèse read the *Life and Letters of Théophane Vénard* (*Vie et Correspondance de Théophane Vénard, 1829–1861*), a French missionary beheaded in Indo-China when only thirty-one, with whom she felt a deep spiritual affinity. In the same month she copied several passages from his letters ('They are my thoughts, my soul resembles his'), which she incorporated later in her own. Thérèse, who did not 'understand saints who don't love their family',[42] found Théophane's last letters, written mainly to his family, especially sympathetic. She copied some short extracts on the back of a picture of the Child Jesus scything lilies:

> . . . I am a spring flower that the Master of the Garden is about to pick for his pleasure. We are all of us flowers planted on this earth, to be picked by God in his own time: a little sooner, a little later. . . . I am a little creature of a day, I go first. One day we shall meet again in Paradise and shall enjoy true happiness . . .[43]

She also wrote a poem to Théophane to commemorate the thirty-sixth anniversary of his beheading. Here she intensified her understanding and use of flowers, sacrifice and suffering by identifying her own approach to them with that of the young martyr:

> Virginal lily, your life had just begun
>> When Jesus heard your loving heart's desire.
> I see in you a flower whose race is run,
>> Yet his hand plucked it but to lift it higher.

And now no longer exile will you know;
    Your ecstasy the blest exult to see.
You rose of love, the Virgin white as snow
    Rejoices in your heavenly purity.
Soldier of Christ, lend me your armour true!
    For sinners' souls I long to give my life;
To shed my tears for them, my blood, like you.
    Protect me then, and arm me for the strife!
I wish to fight for them till life is done,
    God's kingdom take by force, and save their souls.
'Not peace to earth I bring' (so says God's Son),
    'But fire and sword I bear,' and thus consoles.

. . .

I wish to be a fading springtime flower,
    That soon the Lord will gather to his breast!
Come down, dear Théophane, at my last hour;
    Come down for me, sweet youthful martyr blest!
Come with the virginal flames of pure love,
    Come, burn from this my soul all earthly clay,
That I may fly to heaven's courts above,
    And be with God in everlasting day.[44]

On 6 September 1897 she received a relic of Théophane Vénard. During the last weeks of her life she was often observed holding and caressing this and the martyr's portrait, still able thankfully to 'accept / The thorns together with the flowers',[45] as she wrote in 'My Joy!,' a poem for Pauline's feast-day on 21 January 1897. Although she was in a phase of intense spiritual darkness, and within nine months of her agonizing death from tuberculosis, the poem displays her essential trust and therefore optimism:

My peace it is to hide my tears,
  Nor ever show my bitter pain.
What joy to suffer through the years,
  To veil with flowers hurt and strain,
To suffer, yet make no complaint.
  Since this, my Jesus, pleases you,
Could any trial make me faint
  If your cross with flowers I strew?[46]

In this final period, as she thought about examples of martyrdom such as Théophane's, her own illness, and the ultimate purpose of her life, she refined her flower imagery to express her mature understanding of 'littleness':

I must confess that in your letter there is one thing that pains me – namely that you do not know me as I really am. It is true that to find great souls you must come to Carmel; just as in virgin forests there grow flowers of a fragrance and brilliance unknown to the world. Jesus in his mercy has willed that among these flowers smaller ones should grow; never shall I be able to thank him for it enough, for it is owing to this condescension that I, a poor flower of no brilliance, am in the same garden-bed as the roses, my sisters. O my Brother! believe me, I beg you, the good God has not given you a great soul for your sister, but a *very small* and very imperfect one . . .[47]

Whenever May came round and the twenty rose bushes in the cloister courtyard of Carmel blossomed, it was time for the novices to begin their 'liturgy of love' by throwing rose petals at the crucifix at the centre of the garden. Although Thérèse was too ill to take part in the ceremony, she was able to write. Inspired by this event but essentially by the realization that she was facing death, she compared herself to a withered or faded rose that accepts the nature of living and

dying and thereby voluntarily sheds its petals to become nothing in earthly terms. The actual piece was written at the
request of Mother Henriette, a fifty-five-year-old Carmelite
nun in Paris, who was so ill as to be prematurely helpless and
in a state of intense fear, indeed dread, of dying. Thérèse 'put
her whole heart'[48] into the poem, which she produced to
reassure Mother Henriette, who had entered a phase of almost
neurotic scepticism about miracles and the after-life and, it
seems, of more mundane disbelief in Thérèse's literary
abilities as described by Mother Marie de Gonzague when
boasting of her young nun's accomplishments:

> Jesus, when you leave your dear Mother's fond embrace,
>   let go her hand,
> And first, on our hard earth, your little foot must place,
>   Then trembling stand;
> Upon your pathway, fresh rose-leaves I long to spread,
>   An infant's dower,
> So that your tiny feet may very softly tread
>   Upon a flower.
>
> These strewn rose-leaves form the true image of a soul,
>   My Child most dear,
> That longs to sacrifice itself, complete and whole,
>   Each moment here.
> On your blest altars, Lord, fresh roses wish to shine;
>   Radiant, near you,
> They gladly give themselves. Another dream is mine:
>   To fade for you.
>
> How richly graces your feast, dear Child, a rose new-blown,
>   Fragrant and fair.
> But withered roses are forgot, the wild winds' own,
>   Cast anywhere.

Then their scattered leaves seek no earthly joy or wealth;
  For self, no gain.
Little Jesus, I give you all! Nothing of self
  Will now remain.

These roses trampled lie beneath the passer's tread,
  Unmarked, unknown.
I understand their fate: these leaves, though pale and dead,
  Are still your own.
For you they die, as I my time, my life, my all
  For you have spent.
I am seen as a fading rose whose leaves must fall,
  To death consent.

It is for you I die, Jesus, you fairest Fair!
  Joy beyond telling!
Thus, fading, I shall prove my love beyond compare,
  All bliss excelling.
Beneath your steps, your way to ease through earthly night,
  My heart will lie;
Thus, somehow soothing your hard path up Calvary's harsh height,
  I wish to die.[49]

The previously sceptical Mother Henriette was delighted with the poem but wrote to say that surely it needed a final consoling stanza. It should tell how, when the individual died, God would collect the scattered petals to make a beautiful, everlastingly radiant rose. This was contrary to Thérèse's notion of love as complete surrender of self and as trust in God without craving any recompense. She told Sister Marie: 'The good Mother can write her own final couplet along those lines if she likes. I can't see any reason why I should do so. I want to be without petals for ever, to make God happy. Full stop! That's it!'[50]

On 3 June 1897 Mother de Gonzague asked Thérèse to continue her autobiography, and Thérèse returned to the image of the Little Flower, amplifying it in accordance with her developed concept of free will. Her desire to be a flower faded, withered, and unpetalled for some ultimate good did not mean that God would not nurture his plant so that she could make that free choice:

> Jesus knew that his flower was too weak to take root without the life-giving waters of humiliation . . . [but for] some months Jesus has completely changed his method of cultivation. Finding, no doubt, that his little flower has been sufficiently watered, he allows her to grow up under the warm rays of a brilliant sun. He only smiles upon her now. . . . The bright sunlight, far from withering her petals, fosters their growth in a marvellous way. Deep in her calyx she treasures those precious drops of dew, the humiliations of other days, and they remind her always how frail she is . . . her joyful realization [is] that in God's eyes she is a poor worthless thing, and nothing more.[51]

Her idea of self-sacrifice had moved beyond any crude idea of self-punishment, as she told Sister Marie of the Trinity, a novice who wanted to go without Communion to punish herself for some peccadillo:

> Little flower beloved of Jesus, I understand the whole thing perfectly. Realize that it is unnecessary to tell me everything in detail, the *tiny eye* in your calyx shows me what to think of the whole little flower. . . . I am very pleased, very much consoled, but you must no longer *want* to *eat* earth; the forget-me-not need only open, or rather upraise its petals for the Bread of Angels to come like a divine Dew to strengthen it and to give it all it lacks. . . . Good night, poor flowerlet, take my word that I love you more than you think![52]

She recalled her father's gift of the little white flower ten years before,[53] and when Sister Marie of the Sacred Heart told her how sorry they would all be after her death, Thérèse replied: 'Oh no! You will see . . . it will be like a shower of roses,' and added: 'After my death just go to the letter-box and you will find many things to console you.'[54]

Yet again the Child Jesus, flowers, fire and light came together in a typical image-cluster to symbolize her idea of love and reparation: 'May the divine Child Jesus find in your soul a dwelling all fragrant with the roses of Love; may he find the burning lamp of fraternal charity to warm his frozen limbs and rejoice his small heart, making him forget the ingratitude of souls which do not love him enough.'[55]

When Thérèse's condition grew much worse she was taken down to the infirmary on 8 July and stayed there until her death. On the brown curtains about her iron bed she pinned her favourite holy pictures, including those of the Holy Face, Our Lady and 'dear little' Théophane Vénard. The statue of 'Our Lady of the Smile' was brought down to her room where she could see the convent garden through the window.

When Céline offered Thérèse a geranium past its time so that she could scatter its petals at her pictures, Thérèse insisted that only the freshest flowers should be used: 'Never scatter faded flowers . . . only freshly blooming little flowers.'[56] Scattering was not a mere pious but a deeply symbolic action that summed up her offering of her vitality and fullness of life, and the fact that she was content to allow her self to fade and wither.

On 30 July Thérèse's state called for the Last Anointing but the next day she rallied and even joked about the funeral arrangements being made on her behalf. She survived for another two months, sometimes in extreme pain.

On 5 August, the eve of the feast of the Transfiguration, the Sisters removed the picture of the Holy Face from the choir, hung it on the wall near Thérèse's bed, and decorated it with flowers and lights. She quoted Isaiah: 'he shall grow up before him like a tender plant, and as a root out of a dry ground; he hath no form or comeliness; and when we see him there is no beauty. He is despised and rejected of men. . . . Surely he hath borne our griefs, and carried our sorrows,' and said that this was the foundation of her whole piety, for she, too, wished to be 'without beauty . . . unknown to everyone'.[57]

Her desire to be little, like a child, she told Pauline shortly afterwards, was fulfilled because her sole occupation had been to 'gather flowers, the flowers of love and sacrifice', and to offer them to God in order to please him. Being 'little' meant, first, not claiming the credit for one's virtues but realizing that God infused his child with the necessary potential which could always be invoked when needed; and, second, never being discouraged by one's faults, for although children 'often fall they are too little to hurt themselves very much'.[58]

On 14 September Sister Mary of Saint Joseph picked a violet in the garden for Thérèse, who looked at it and exclaimed: 'Ah! The scent of violets!' It was only one of the many flowers sent to her by friends outside the convent.[59]

When people brought her roses to cheer her up, she enacted her notion of herself 'as a fading rose whose leaves must fall' by removing each petal gently to stand for everything she had willingly surrendered, before touching it to Jesus' wounds on her crucifix, and letting it fall. As the petals slipped from her bed to the floor, she told the Sisters 'quite seriously' to gather every single one since they would help them to 'perform favours later'.[60] When Mother Agnes asked her to scatter flowers on the Sisters as they stood round her bed, Thérèse's reply stressed the profound personal significance of casting flowers, and the importance of the language of flowers to the symbolism through which she both interpreted and expressed the ultimate meaning of her life and her relationship to God: 'Please don't ask me to do that. I don't want to scatter flowers on people. I would do it for the Blessed Virgin or St Joseph but I won't scatter them on any other creatures.'[61] She showed that this implied no lack of concern for the natural world and for all sentient things when her bed was rolled out under the cloister and Sister Marie of the Sacred Heart, in charge of the courtyard garden, was about to pull out a dying rhododendron shoot. Thérèse exclaimed: 'Oh, Sister Marie . . . I don't understand you. . . . I am about to die. For my sake, spare the life of this poor rhododendron.'[62]

As the end approached, Thérèse recast her anticipation of heaven in terms of her happiest childhood days: 'I want to run through the fields of heaven . . . where the grass is green for ever and ever, with beautiful flowers that never fade, and lovely angel children.'[63] When Sister Teresa of Saint Augustine visited her and talked of the 'glory' soon to be hers, Thérèse refined her vision of simple childlike joy by insisting that even in heaven she wished to be a 'little nothing'; no more, in fact, than the pinch of greenery between the splendid blooms in the celestial Gardener's final bouquet.

In her testimony Céline drew on Thérèse's own words to describe her life as that of a loving person 'strewing the petals of her flowers, her sacrifices before Jesus', and of someone finally able to ask: 'Why should death make me afraid? Anything I have ever done was for God.'[64]

According to Céline, Thérèse's last recorded words (on Thursday, 30 September 1897) were: 'All right, then! Let it go on. . . . Oh! I would not want to suffer less!' and, as she looked at her crucifix: 'Oh! . . . I love him, My God . . . I love . . . you!'.[65] Then she gazed intently at a spot just above Our Lady's statue for a few moments, closed her eyes, and died.

~♣ 4 ♣~

1 October 1897 to the Present

God sows chaste flowers to light us on our way.

Victor Hugo

Our Lord loves the glad of heart, the children that greet him with a smile.
I would not mind how much I suffered if I could make God smile, even once.

Thérèse of Lisieux

Distilling: A Heavenly Mission

Thérèse lived in obscurity. She was and remains an enactment of Jesus' parable of the mustard seed: 'The kingdom of heaven is like a tiny grain of mustard seed which a man took and sowed in his field. As a seed it is the smallest of them all, but it grows to be the biggest of all plants' (Matt. 13: 31–3).

In the last year of her life, she called herself 'a little seed' from which 'no one knows yet what will develop'.[1] With the posthumous publication of *Story of a Soul*, and with the subsequent interventions acknowledged by millions of people, the 'little seed' developed beyond all expectations. In many ways, the continued flowering of Thérèse, her reception over more than a century, is the most extraordinary aspect of her story.

'A little labour today, eternal rest tomorrow' were the words inscribed on the wall she passed as she ascended every night to her cell in the Lisieux Carmel. Yet Thérèse believed that her death would be the start of her mission to priests and sinners everywhere: her showers of roses – shed through her self-abandonment to God – that would help struggling plants to grow to their intended simple beauty in Jesus' garden. On 30 July 1896 she wrote to Father Roulland, before his depart-ure for the Far East: 'Good-bye, Brother ... distance can never separate our souls, death will only make our union closer. If I go to Heaven soon, I will ask Jesus' permission to visit you at Su-Chuen, we shall continue our apostolate together.'[2] Thérèse believed that the desires God has put in us foreshadow an as yet unsuspected grace in the future. She was sure that the last-minute 'conversion' of the criminal Pranzini was a sign that her prayers had been heard and answered, and looked on him as her 'first child'.[3]

She also thought that angels, divinely-created immortal spirits, are concerned for our welfare, help to safeguard it, yet suffer no reduction of their focus on God. This assured her that her intuition about an active life hereafter was cor-rect. If angels were active in eternity, then God would surely want Thérèse to work for mortal beings until the final transformation of all mortality into immortality.

A reading in the refectory in May/June 1897 from the Life of Saint Aloysius Gonzaga reinforced her conviction that the brevity of her life on earth would not diminish the fruitfulness of her life in heaven. A passage in the Life prompted Thérèse's famous phrase 'a shower of roses' and the associated train of thought. Thérèse found Aloysius interesting though 'extra-ordinary' and not wholly to her taste. He had entered the Jesuit novitiate house of Sant'Andrea in Rome when only eighteen, suffered from delicate health made worse by savage mortification of the flesh, and died a few months before his twenty-fourth birthday. When in Milan, he had had a revelation of his imminent death, which, after nursing plague victims in Rome, he accepted with joy: 'We are going, father . . . !' 'Where?' asked his provincial. 'To heaven,' Aloysius replied.[4]

The incident in the Life that impressed Thérèse came from the story of a sick German monk who asked Aloysius to heal him, and was vouchsafed an apparition of the saint and a shower of roses on the monk's bed as a sign of his eventual recovery. After hearing this episode, Thérèse told her god-mother during the 9 June recreation: 'I shall bring down a shower of roses after my death.'[5] The initial location of Thérèse's roses, in the sense of cures and favours attributed to her, was the symbolic paradise of Carmel itself.

After Thérèse's death, her body was laid out behind the choir grating at Carmel. Visitors were allowed to view her remains through it. Sister Vincent de Paul, now sorry that she had once spoken unkindly to Thérèse, knelt by the bier, pressed her forehead to it, and was overwhelmingly assured that her long-standing cerebral anaemia had vanished.

Immediately after Thérèse's death, a nun among those present smelled a very strong scent of violets; two days later a child in the crowd filing past the grating noticed the rich odour of lilies – though Thérèse's remains were decorated with artificial flowers. Thereafter reports multiplied of mys-terious scents of flowers rising from spots in the convent where flowers had never been placed. These were ascribed to Thérèse.[6]

On Monday, 4 October 1897, Thérèse was buried in the town cemetery, in a simple grave with a wooden cross inscribed thus: 'I want to spend my heaven doing good on earth.'

When a member of a Carmelite community died, the con-vent sent a notice to all the other houses of the Order. The obituary of Thérèse used for this purpose was the *Story of a*

Soul, which helped the details of her example and resolutions to spread to the point of fame.

Isidore Guérin, Thérèse's uncle, commissioned a provincial publisher, Saint-Paul in Bar-le-Duc, to issue the book. Monsieur Guérin undertook to pay the costs, and corrected the proofs. The book was 475 pages long; the print run 2,000 copies; and it cost 4 francs. It appeared on 30 September 1898, a year after Thérèse's death. It was sent to Carmelite convents, to monasteries and convents of other, like-minded Orders, to ecclesiastics, and to selected 'people in the world'. By the end of October 1898, letters about the book were reaching the Lisieux Carmel. From January 1899, appreciations started to arrive from around the world: from the Saint-Louis (USA) Carmel; from Sydney (Australia); and from Vietnam. The first printing was exhausted by the beginning of 1899. Copies were borrowed and passed on, and Thérèse's story spread by word of mouth.

Readers not only praised the book but recorded various encounters with Thérèse and their assurance that she had intervened or would intervene for them. A feeling of closeness to her and belief in her apparent promises inspired the phenomenal growth of Thérèse's popularity among ordinary people. She was 'their sort of person', whom they could confide in and who would understand their problems, even when these were distant from her recorded experience. Unlike other, seemingly remote intercessors, the Thérèse who talked to them as simply and directly as she did to her Sisters and to Jesus, would certainly sympathize with them.

More and more letters testifying to Thérèse's interventions were received. In 1898, for example, Father Grange of Caen commended the Sisters for publishing the book: '. . . even when she was on her deathbed, I asked Thérèse to grant a favour for the success of my vocation. This was granted . . . I went to pray at her grave . . . and I took away a little pebble, a flower and a fragment of the cross'.[7] The purloining of flowers from the grave became a problem. By 1912 a permanent notice said: 'Visitors removing flowers are requested to leave the roots.'

Sister Marie Estelle of Riom told Pauline: 'I am old, but, Mother, believe me, as I turned the pages of this book I became my energetic twenty-year-old self once again.'[8] A Madame Tostain reminded her:

> You will remember, Mother, that a few days after Thérèse's death, I wrote to say that I . . . wondered if Thérèse really still existed in any way . . . But the story of Thérèse's life has been of immense benefit to me. She suffered like me but did not question anything and submitted to the trials God sent her. . . . I now regularly consult Thérèse and talk to her constantly.[9]

The formation of the Thérèse cult was already under way and soon became an international phenomenon. Translations of her autobiography appeared from 1899 onwards, and a second French edition was exhausted in a few months.

In 1902 Mother Agnes issued a 'popular' edition consisting of twelve chapters of *Story of a Soul* and entitled *Une rose effeuillée* (A Rose without its Petals). In 1904, the monastery offered an 'illustrated publicity edition' entitled *Appel aux petites âmes* (A Call to Ordinary Souls) at 25 centimes each, with a free copy for every twelve ordered, and 18 francs for a hundred copies. The range of inexpensive editions and association items expanded year by year. *Pensées de Soeur Thérèse de l'Enfant Jésus* (Thoughts of Sister Thérèse of the Child Jesus), along with twenty of her poems, was published in 1908. A Thérèse calendar, bearing a rose petal to be peeled off for each day of the year, appeared in 1910.

Correspondents asked for photographs and other images of the 'Little Sister'. Before long, 'relics' (objects that had belonged to Thérèse or had been in contact with her or her remains) were in demand. The dissemination of Thérèse's image was a major factor in promoting her posthumous reception. Thérèse's sister Céline, Sister Geneviève, was an 'artist',[10] and had been granted permission to keep her camera in the convent. She took numerous photographs of Thérèse: as a sacristan, in her dramatic role as Joan of Arc, at the foot of the cross in the courtyard, washing the laundry, and so on. This, however, was still the period in which many people thought that only a drawn or painted portrait was an authentic likeness and could reveal something of a subject's true nature.

The first edition of *Story of a Soul* included a decorative frontispiece based on Céline's photograph of Thérèse, on 7 June 1897, holding the images of the Child Jesus and the Holy Face. She had a high fever at the time, could scarcely kneel, and told Céline 'to be quick as she felt exhausted'.[11] The frontispiece photograph needed a nine-seconds exposure time, and Thérèse screwed up her face to keep a steady pose. Her real smile disappeared.

Céline's first painting of Thérèse (1899) showed her with the gospel on her heart and her hands about to pluck the chords of a harp, so that the portrait expressed her life as a hymn of sacred love in a Carmelite version of the theme of St Cecilia and the power of music.

For the second edition of the autobiography, Céline made a charcoal sketch after a photograph of 1894. This became the 'official' portrait of Thérèse. In 1923 a light appeared round her head to signify her beatification. In 1925 this became a halo to celebrate her canonization.

Céline produced a whole series of portraits. The most popular was that of Thérèse with roses (1912). Flowers became a favourite adjunct of many reworked images of Thérèse, from her first Communion portrait, in which she wears a veil crowned with roses, to imaginary portrayals of her apparitions bearing roses. Among Thérèse's many references to flowers, those associated with favours granted after her death impressed many readers, especially those whose awareness of her came only from holy pictures bearing a single quotation or a conflation of her words.

The sense of these passages was easily associated or confused with an occasion, as when (in her 'Canticle' of September 1896) she used floral imagery to express her resolve to love Jesus in the very least things: 'I, the little one, shall strew flowers and perfume the Divine Throne with their fragrance . . . these flowers will be each word and look, each little daily sacrifice. . . . I want to suffer and rejoice for Love's sake, and that is how I shall strew my flowers.'[12]

Thérèse's references to the Child Jesus, sometimes even those to his sowing or gathering flowers, were now associated with the scattering of flowers as the fulfilment of Thérèse's promise to do good on earth. Ecclesiastical illustrators and their advisers evidently found it difficult to interpret Thérèse's intercessions appropriately. One very popular image was a painting representing the Child Jesus escaping from his mother's arms to welcome Thérèse kneeling on the doorstep and strewing rose petals. The front endpapers of the 1926 English *A Little White Flower* show Thérèse kneeling on a cloud praying to the Child Jesus seated on a somewhat higher cloud. In an attempt at theological correctness, Jesus lets down a shower of roses, some of which are caught on Thérèse's cloud, while the main flow continues down to Earth. The 1947 edition of Thomas Taylor's *Saint Thérèse of Lisieux, the Little Flower of Jesus* contains a sepia reproduction of a pre-war gouache of Our Lady and the Child Jesus seated on a cloud immediately above St Peter's and the Vatican. Thérèse kneels at a lower point on the same cloud, her eyes raised to the mother and Child. In one hand she receives roses one by one from the hands of Jesus, who takes them from

Mary's lap; with the other hand she drops them on an empty St Peter's Square.

Some attempts to reconcile Thérèse's pronouncements with received doctrine resulted in adjustments of her actual statements. She had said that she would scatter roses and return to this world, but some authorities thought she should be shown merely petitioning God, who would cause the roses to descend. Similarly, invocations of Thérèse ought to have asked her to pray for the petitioner. As the abundant evidence in chapels and churches shows, many who sought her help asked her to grant the cure or thanked her for the examination result, and so on, without mentioning God. Some official measures unintentionally encouraged this tendency. For instance, on 10 June 1915 Pope Benedict XV authorized the striking of a Thérèse medal, and insisted that it must not be blessed and that no statue or image of her was to be associated with images of Christ, Our Lady or the saints, because she was not yet beatified.

On the walls of the chapel adjacent to Thérèse's birthplace in Alençon, 'R.M.S.' acknowledges that 'The fragrant petals of the Shower of Roses promised by Sister Thérèse have fallen on us'; 'R.' records his or her 'Faithful and thankful love for my heavenly Protectress'; 'R.' promises 'Constant evidence of our thanks to our heavenly Nurse'; a father from the Doubs commemorates 'A mother and her little daughter both cured by the THAUMATURGE'; 'J.C.' tells posterity that 'The "Little Queen" has made a "rose" flower on our patient and worked the cure we asked her for.' On the walls of the Carmelite church at Lisieux, 'an Italian soldier' gives 'grateful thanks to Sister Thérèse of Lisieux'; Madame Genty as 'A grandmother gratefully acknowledges the SAINT's unmistakable protection of her soldier grandsons'; a 'poor and grateful sinner' declares that 'Sister Thérèse has saved my soul and my honour'; 'P.H.R.' thanks 'You, Sister Thérèse, in the name of your faithful servants of Auchieta College and your ardent Brazilian Legion'; 'E.B.' testifies that 'The little SAINT of Carmel cured me of a cancerous tumour and never ceases to protect me'; 'F.G.' gives thanks to 'Dear little Thérèse', because 'You have clearly watched over us! Always keep us under your heavenly protection'; and 'M.V.' thanks 'Thérèse, the beautiful "rose" of CARMEL, who established and blessed my household.'[13]

The most influential drawing of Thérèse with roses, in which she holds a crucifix and a gathering of roses, some falling to the ground, first appeared in the 1914 edition of *Story of a Soul*. In 1925 Céline produced a colour version of the same subject, and corrected the supposed faults of the first attempt: 'I put all my heart into it. . . . It seemed that my Thérèse was actually looking at me. In my opinion, it is her best likeness.'[14] This edition contained an 'introduction to the portraits', followed by a note observing that the portrayal of Thérèse as rose-carrier reproduced her chosen form of apparition in various reported visions. Thérèse's roses were scarcely ever shown as thorny, however, although she had said: 'I shall sing even if I have to gather my flowers among thorns, and the longer and sharper the thorns, the more melodious my song will be.'[15]

★　★　★

Thérèse's flowers, especially her promised shower of roses, were raised to a new level of significance in 1903 when a young Scottish priest made a momentous suggestion. Father Thomas Taylor visited Lisieux, met Thérèse's sisters, and advised them to start the process of petitions and applications for her canonization. The Carmelites were astonished. Nothing in Thérèse's life seemed to justify the long, arduous and expensive procedure of gathering and presenting testimonies. Eventually, the Lisieux Sisters were convinced that the seemingly immense effort called for had some chance of succeeding.

Although the traditional evidence-gathering and miracle-recording required for beatification and canonization took up much of the Sisters' and associates' time, the fast-growing recognition of Thérèse's effectiveness as a petitioner in heaven or miracle-worker on earth was the main force behind the rapid advance of her cause.

When Thérèse's coffin was opened on 6 September 1910, her body had not proved incorruptible. According to Dr La Néele, a cousin of the Martin sisters present at the exhumation, only the bones were intact. He removed some fragments of her habit, and the still wholesome palm buried with her, gave her rosary cross to the Bishop of Bayeux and Lisieux, and clothed her in a new habit and veil. He placed bouquets of flowers in the coffin, which was enclosed in a lead outer casing. She was reburied in a new grave nearby.[16]

As more and more copies of Thérèse's autobiography were sold, the visitors to her grave made her as attractive, for those in search of flowers spiritual and in kind, as the Curé d'Ars, who was so popular in his own lifetime that the French railway companies timetabled special trains for penitents. In 1913, the on-the-spot reporter for one review noted that the 'Holy Spirit was breathing' with unusual favour on the Lisieux cemetery, for the superintendent estimated the number of pilgrims from all over the world at more than three hundred a day during the holiday months. Every class of society was represented, 'from the devout poor who come on foot, to the rich whose cars queue up at the cemetery gate as if outside some great house where a fashionable reception is being held'. The grave was 'covered with white flowers and the faded blooms have to be taken away every morning'.[17] As Bishop de Teil, Vice-Postulator of the cause, remarked when calming anxious Sisters: 'The two most important factors in a canonization are money and miracles. Sister Thérèse is providing us plentifully with both!'[18]

Thérèse's extraordinary attraction for all sorts and conditions of people did not go unremarked by the Vatican between her death and canonization. These were times of vast changes – in popular franchise, culture, manners and morals – and soon of world war and political revolutions. Every flower scattered by Thérèse strengthened the appeal of a Church challenged by social and political movements. The initial reception of Thérèse as thaumaturge and future saint depended on her autobiography and on popular piety but also on the development of the Church's attitude to potentially influential intercessors.

In Thérèse's lifetime, especially in the 1870s, the Church learned how to select cults in accordance with universally advantageous criteria, to assimilate them, and to direct religious orders to promote and organize them, partly in response to political trends that signalled the growth of new threats to belief, practice and the Church as an establishment.

The possibility of a direct assault on the French Church was brutally evident under the Paris Commune in 1870. The Communards were ferociously suppressed by a regime that did not slaughter archbishops or nuns but was intent on replacing the Church's influence in civil life with secular institutions. The isolation of the papacy, and the reduction of its secular power and of its influence over nominal Catholics during the Risorgimento and after Italian unification, evoked the most thoroughgoing changes in Church strategy.

Ecclesiastical attitudes to publicity techniques and to such technological facilities of the modern world as the railways, which various popes had condemned and rejected during the first two thirds of the nineteenth century, changed completely. Examples of a new strategy of response to and anticipation of such political trends, and of the social indifference to, or changes in, religious belief and observance which they revealed, were the promotion of Pompeii in Italy, Knock in

Ireland, Pontmain in France, and the official ecclesiastical encouragement of the cult of Our Lady of Lourdes and of St Bernadette, the enhancement of Lourdes as an apparition site, the facilitation of mass rallies and of pilgrimages to it, and a new proficiency in recording miraculous cures there.[19]

The rift between the French State and the Vatican widened in the 1890s and early 1900s and culminated in the virtual disestablishment of the French Church under Pius X. Suitable new cults became desirable means of support for the official Church. The nascent cult of Thérèse of Lisieux was rather different from most of those centred on Marian apparitions. Thérèse did not act as a channel of revelations or injunctions from Our Lady. She was not an illiterate or semi-literate peasant girl. There was no need to assign a specific religious Order to organize her cult and pilgrimages, or to build a basilica. The Carmelites were already available and at work on her cause.

Moreover, Thérèse's writings evoked and maintained her reception much as Mary's reported pronouncements had done in the apparition-cults of the last quarter of the nineteenth century. Thérèse recorded her devotion to Mary but the main relationship was between herself and God. She had attended school for no more than five years, yet she was well educated when compared with the non-Martin members of her Carmel, and even with many priests of the time. She belonged to the urban lower-middle to middle class – to the 'rising bourgeoisie'. Although the Carmelite Order followed an enclosed obedience, it already had a worldwide structure, and to this day it remains the organizing body for the propagation of devotion to Thérèse as one of a company of Carmelite saints. All these factors encouraged an emphasis on certain aspects of Thérèse's spirituality to the neglect of others; and especially on her 'roses' conceived of as miraculous actions, rather than on her central conception of herself as a 'little flower'.

The official Church did not restructure, or 'Marianize', the reaction to Thérèse as an outstanding religious figure in her own right, but recognized its strength, rapid spread and utility. Cardinal Vico of the Sacred Congregation of Rites noted that the Vatican would be well advised to speed up the 'glorification' of the 'Little Saint', or the 'voice of the nations would be heard ahead of it'. Petitions for Thérèse's formal recognition arrived from all over the world. Gifts such as that from Brazil of a gold processional reliquary enhanced with precious stones came to Lisieux. The number of pilgrims recorded annually at the tomb there increased from 80,000 to 300,000. Letters to Lisieux reported thousands of miracles ascribed to Thérèse. Spectacular flowers were strewn when the first official public acknowledgement, the beatification, was immediately followed by a host of ever more impressive cures.

The remains of Thérèse's first interment reburied by her cousin in 1910 were officially authenticated in 1917. On 26 March 1923, attended by 50,000 pilgrims, they were solemnly translated to Lisieux itself. A correspondent of the newspaper *Nouvelliste de Rennes* remarked that 'fragrant emanations of roses and violets floated up from the open grave'.[20] Many of those present testified to their personal experience of the traditional odour of sanctity, but associated it with specific flowers. The connection between Thérèse's 'actual' flowers and her flower-favours was cited as the cause when a woman from Angers placed her paralytic child on the coffin, and the little girl jumped down immediately, joined the procession, and began to sing. Three more cures were recorded during the coffin's passage.

On 17 May 1925, twenty-seven years after her death, eight years after being declared venerable, and two years after beatification, Thérèse was canonized in St Peter's before a congregation of 50,000 out of 200,000 applicants. Prelates, priests and religious processed down the aisle before Thérèse's banner under garlands of roses, which were now universally acknowledged to be the central, many-aspected symbol of her aspirations and mission. When five white roses floated down, described a great curve in the air, and came to rest at the Pope's feet, it was suggested that the Saint herself had made a characteristic response to the pomp and ceremony, and to the oddly inappropriate accompaniments of a canonization, such as the cardinals' offerings of decorated candles, of silver- or gilt-caged turtle-doves and pigeons, and of wine and water encased in precious metals.

★ ★ ★

Perfuming: A Shower of Roses

At 2 a.m. on 17 July 1897, Thérèse had coughed up blood and said: 'I feel . . . that my mission is about to begin, my mission of making God loved as I love him, of giving my little way to souls.' She was sure that: 'If God answers my desires, my heaven will be spent on earth until the end of the world. . . . I want to spend my heaven in doing good on earth.'[21]

She had already said that she was sure that Jesus would never refuse her anything in heaven, because on earth she had never denied him anything he had demanded of her since she was three. On 14 July 1897 she had written to Father Adolphe Roulland, a missionary in China and her second 'spiritual brother': '. . . you will not have time to send me the list of things I can do for you in heaven, but I guess them; and in any event you will have but to whisper them and I shall hear you.'[22]

On 18 July 1897, Thérèse told her first cousin, Marie Guérin (Sister Marie of the Eucharist), when asked if she could 'obtain great graces for [Marie] when she was in heaven': 'Oh! when I am in heaven, I will do very many things, great things . . . when I am up there, I will follow you very closely!' When Marie said this would frighten her, Thérèse's response was: 'Does your guardian angel frighten you? He follows you . . . all the time; well, I will follow you in the same way, and even closer!'[23]

The main impression Thérèse's floral language left on the religious sensibilities of an ever-increasing public was that of a determination to help suffering humanity. Fewer people saw her as recommending her 'little way' and thus helping them to develop an appropriate religious attitude and practice.

Attempts to quantify and classify miracles in response to petitions to saints during the ages of faith agree roughly with the following list for the eleventh and twelfth centuries (in descending order of frequency): cures and revivals, visions, punishments, favourable interventions, protection from dangers, freeing of prisoners, canonization of a saint, prediction and telepathy, conception of a child. The first category, with about sixty per cent of the total, predominates.[24]

The same group was also to the fore with regard to Thérèse's effective intercessions and interventions in the most intensively recorded period, that between her death and canonization. Most people were convinced that she would help them to overcome, first, physical and mental infirmity; second, problems caused by inadequate funds or abilities; and, third, religious or moral difficulties.

The shower of roses that Thérèse had promised to let fall after her death came to mean miracles in answer to appeals for her help. These invocations usually took the form of a novena, or prayers repeated over nine days for a special purpose, for which recommended, and later officially-approved, devotions in honour of Thérèse were soon available.

Testimonies, or a 'trail of roses and perfumes'

The increasingly predominant notion of Thérèse's roses is shown in the language used by one passionate advocate of her cause: '. . . the more her power with God is revealed to men, the more will they invoke her, and the better will she promote his glory by "doing good upon earth" . . . the perfume of the "roses" will draw hearts along her simple pathway to Heavenly Heights.'[25] As people began to invoke Thérèse's help, miracles of healing of the kind obtained from powerful intercessors over thousands of years were recorded.

In 1907, in preparation for her beatification and eventual canonization, the Carmelites of Lisieux published the first of seven volumes of accounts of miracles attributed to Thérèse. Entitled *Pluie de roses* (A Rain of Roses), the expanded series amounted to 3,000 pages when the last volume was issued in 1925. These volumes testify to healings and favours obtained for people of all ages and from all parts of the world. They were ascribed to Thérèse's intercession or, very often, to her direct action.

Some cures happened after fervent prayer to Thérèse; others after placing a relic – a clipping from her hair, a piece of her clothing, a bone splinter, even a fragment of her childhood letters destroyed by her sisters on Bishop Teil's advice – on an infected area of a person's body, under a pillow, or near the bed; yet others by crumbling or mashing a relic or memento into water or a cordial and consuming it. Sachets containing earth from beneath her first coffin, wood from her bed-planks and the floor of her cell, or threads from her pillow, bed-curtains, outer clothes or underwear were obtainable long before her beatification. Some 17,500,000 relics and 30,500,000 pictures of Thérèse were distributed between 1897 and 1925, and most early accounts of her miracles show that supplicants possessed or were given a portrait or relic of her.

Whereas most interventions amounted to healing of physical or mental illness, in some cases Thérèse helped people in kind, or financially. Some individuals reporting personal miracles were sure they were touched by Thérèse, who visited them in a dream or when they were awake. Parents or relatives interceded for a sick child; communities for religious, especially when nuns wished only for God's will to be done and did not request a cure. A subsequent recovery led to a life-long devotion to their benefactress.

Actual roses or their scent accompanied many cures, as in the case of Sister Louise de Saint Germain (Sister Aloysia), dying of stomach ulcers in a convent at the foot of the Pyrenees. A petition to Thérèse elicited not only a vision of the intercessor herself and, some days later, a complete recovery, but multicoloured rose petals strewn round the patient's bed. Such supernatural events were unmistakable evidence of the fulfilment of Thérèse's intention:

> To scatter flowers for You, sacrifice
> My smallest sign and my intensest dread,
> My sorrows, bliss, renunciations, joys –
> Behold, here are my roses, white and red![26]

Examples from each of the main categories of Thérèse's rose-miracles, which secured her beatification and canonization, will show how people conceived of her and her association with flowers.

Roses and perfumes
In the early years of her cause several manifestations of Thérèse focused on flowers were reported to the Lisieux Carmel or to priests.

A BUSHEL OF ROSES   Mrs Stuart of Philadelphia, an invalid for more than twenty years, joined in the novena preceding Thérèse's canonization on 17 May 1925. She struggled out to the six o'clock Mass in St Patrick's Church but had a stroke on the way, and died when taken home. Her daughter Mary prayed for a sign that her mother was in heaven, a 'dream of her or of the Little Flower. That night the perfume of roses was perceived in the house.' On 18 May the family realized 'Little Thérèse [was] in the room when they smelled a "most wonderful scent of roses . . . like a gust of wind", which that night grew as strong as a "whole bushel of roses".'The younger daughter opened the drawer of the sewing-machine and found a 'little rosebud, fresh as if newly plucked from a rose-bush'. The 'rose from heaven' was placed in a watchcase. Four months later the figure of a little head appeared on one petal and that of a sorrowful face on another. The clergy submitted the rosebud to three experts who confirmed that it was of an entirely unknown variety. More than 100,000 pilgrims visited the house, and the rose was often used to help sick people. It was still fresh more than a year later, and 'both the exquisitely beautiful face of the child and the profile of the man in agony [were] beyond doubt woven in the texture of the flower itself.'[27]

Cures of members of Religious Orders

CURE OF A STOMACH ULCER   On 25 July 1909, Sister Marie-Benigne of the Visitation Monastery at Caen informed the Lisieux Carmel that from December 1908 she had suffered from a stomach ulcer, like a 'wild animal . . . devouring my stomach', which prevented her from walking or eating solids and made her vomit blood four or five times a day. The Sisters began a novena to Sister Thérèse on 24 June and on the last day Sister Frances-Teresa (Léonie Martin) gave her a little water containing a rose petal which Thérèse had touched to her crucifix. 'From that moment I no longer felt any pain . . . at breakfast, I was served like the rest of the community; I ate some omelette, some peas, and some salad . . . I am today in the best of health.' The doctor's certificate confirmed the disappearance of the ulcer.[28]

Cures of priests

Thérèse said that she wanted to help priests after her death. Multiple cures of priests were ascribed to this intention.

CURE OF A TUBERCULAR LUNG   On 7 March 1909 Doctor La Néele (Thérèse's cousin) reported that from 1905 Abbé Charles Anne, a Lisieux seminarist, had suffered from tubercular lesions of both lungs, an essentially incurable condition treated in the pre-antibiotic era only by long rest in a sanatorium in, preferably, an Alpine area. In 1906 the diagnosis was confirmed by isolation of the TB bacillus, and death was imminent. The priest's parents said a novena to ask Our Lady of Lourdes for a cure through the intercession of Sister Thérèse, and the seminarist wore a sachet containing some of her hair on his chest. They then began another novena, asking only Thérèse for a cure, and promising to publish an account of it. The next day the fever and the cavities disappeared. The doctor was 'stupefied' to see Charles still alive, and years later confirmed his excellent health and a scientifically inexplicable recovery from the 'gravest galloping consumption, before which the doctor is powerless'.[29]

Cures of people after others' petitions

CURE OF A MISSIONARY NUN INTENT ON DYING   The Prioress of the Carmel of Mangalore, East Indies, wrote to the Lisieux Carmelites on 7 June 1909 with the news that 'your little Sister, who so much loved the missionary Carmelites, has deigned to favour us by one of her visits'. The doctor was sure that Sister Mary of the Calvary, suffering from pneumonia, liver and kidney disease, and spitting fragments of lung, would be dead within the next night. She herself wanted only to die and told two physicians that any further treatment would be contrary to God's designs. Then the convent received the Lisieux circular 'relating the wonderful things done by the powerful intervention before God of your dear little Saint'. After a novena, Sister Mary experienced 'something which cannot be explained', when alone and wide awake yet 'suspended in space', and asked: 'What more for the glory of God, for the Holy Church, for your Holy Order and your community, than if the miracle of your cure was to hasten the glorification of Sister Thérèse of the Child Jesus!' At once she replied: 'No, I do not desire any longer to die. I am going to pray and to begin a novena.' She was given a picture of Thérèse and placed it near her pillow. Within two days she had got up, dressed, received Communion, sang one of Thérèse's hymns, and resumed her work as portress, 'radiant with gratitude and love'.[30]

Cures of children

A CURE OF KERATITIS   On 7 December 1908, Dr La Néele recorded the recovery from acute keratitis at Lisieux on 26 May 1908 of Reine Fauquet, a girl aged four-and-a-half, who had lost her sight. The infant-class teacher advised the mother to ask Sister Thérèse for a cure, to carry the child to Thérèse's grave, and to be especially confident since Thérèse's father had called her 'Reine' (Queen). After reading the abridged life of Thérèse the mother asked for a novena of prayers at the Carmel and lit a candle to the Blessed Virgin in honour of Sister Thérèse. On returning home, Reine cried out: 'Mother . . . I can see just as well as you.' The doctor declared her completely cured. The girl's nine-year-old sister revealed later that Reine had said: 'I saw my little Thérèse, over there, quite close to my bed. She took my hand, and smiled at me. She was beautiful; she had a veil and it was all bright round her head.'[31]

Cures of people of other nationalities

Most of the early miracles worked by Thérèse were reported from France, then from other Latin countries, but the worldwide spread of Carmelite houses and the dissemination of translations of *Story of a Soul* soon brought a succession of cures from the English-speaking countries.

CURE OF MRS DORANS Mrs Dorans was a Glasgow widow who for eleven years, never sleeping for more than seven minutes, had suffered continual pain from an inoperable and proliferative tumour of the left side. By 22 August 1909 she had taken no solid food for ten weeks and was on the point of dying. Priests, religious and friends had made novenas to the Sacred Heart, Our Lady of Lourdes, St Joseph and her favourite saints. A friend suggested a novena in honour of the Little Flower, but Mrs Dorans was reluctant to show lack of faith in the Sacred Heart, Our Lady, and St Joseph, so a compromise was reached: Thérèse would be asked to pray to them for a cure. After four days into the novena, she slept quietly, was awakened by a light touch on the shoulders, felt a 'sweet warm breath', and knew that the 'dear little sister had come from heaven to spend a few moments with her'. She went to sleep and, when she awoke, found that the 'terrible swelling had completely disappeared'. The doctor acknowledged that 'a higher power had worked this cure', and certified this 'inexplicable recovery'.[32]

CURE OF MARY ANTES On 12 August 1909, Sister Antonia of the Dominican Convent of Holy Cross, New York, reported the cure of her sister, Mary Antes, who had been trampled by a frightened horse on 30 July. She had a pierced lung and injured heart. The hospital abandoned all hope. On 3 August a 'religious, very devout to Sister Thérèse of the Child Jesus, advised us to put all our hope in her. . . . I gave my sister a picture-relic of the little saint; she laid it with the greatest confidence on her crushed body.' By the last day of the novena the sick girl had recovered.[33]

SISTER THÉRÈSE AMONG THE CANNIBALS   Conversion of non-Catholics was a prime aim, however, and some singular instances were ascribed to Thérèse's missionary endeavours in the early years of her cause. On 30 September 1911, Father Bertreux wrote from the Solomon Islands about the experiences of his assistant, Father Coicaud, who had found the cannibals of Malaita 'difficult to deal with'. After four weeks 'he was surprised his head was still on his shoulders', for the chief had no idea how many people he had helped to roast and eat, although:

> he knows for certain that he has killed twelve people with his own hand. Scarcely a year ago he killed one of his daughters to annoy one of his wives. But he is a changed man since Sister Thérèse worked his conversion. 'All that is over now,' he declared. And when his little girl was baptized – the first baptism on the island – he called her Thérèse . . . when Father Coicaud went to Mala for the first time, I gave him two of her relics: one he placed in his hut, and the other he cast on the island. Thérèse is therefore in Mala; can we wonder that there are already forty Catholics on the island?[34]

Cures of old people

RECONSTRUCTION OF A TONGUE   Ferdinand Aubry at the Home for the Aged, kept by the Little Sisters of the Poor at Lisieux, had suffered a stroke, could hardly speak, and developed a gangrenous ulceration of the tongue, which became so enormous he could not close his mouth. The Little Sisters invoked Thérèse and brought him her picture and a relic. The Mother Superior read out the passage in *Story of a Soul* where Thérèse speaks of a poor old sick man whom she wished to befriend, when a child, by taking alms to him. A novena was started, two Sisters made a pilgrimage to Thérèse's tomb, but Aubry's tongue began to split up. The

Sisters asked the Carmelites for a petal of the roses with which Sister Thérèse had 'perfumed her crucifix upon her death-bed', and put the relic near the old man, in a sealed bag. He broke the seal and swallowed the petal. 'He declared suddenly, "I am cured." "Since when?" asked the Sister. "Two days ago." ' Within three weeks even his mutilated tongue was restored 'with the same volume, the same form, the same consistency, and the same colour, without any line of separation by which the new part could be distinguished'.[35]

Instantaneous cures

CURE OF SPINAL DISEASE   Madame M. S. had been ill for four years and could scarcely walk. In December 1910 a specialist diagnosed spinal sclerosis of the spinal marrow and imminent total paralysis and blindness. Other doctors suspected a tumour affecting the spine and advised a long course of radiation, with side-effects and no result under six months. Treatment began on 15 March 1911, with only slight improvement. On 10 April she was given a relic of Sister Thérèse and started a novena to the 'little saint in union with the Carmelite Convent of Lisieux'. On 13 April she moved the relic along her spine – at once she was able to walk 'without support, quite naturally, and without the slightest fatigue: The little saint had then instantly cured her! . . . She was able to make her Easter Communion in the church.'[36]

Cures with rose petals

On 23 January 1903 Abbé D. Petit, Curé of Marnes-la-Coquette, wrote to the Carmel of Lisieux to describe the cure of Jouanne, a gardener's wife operated on for a strangulated hernia more than a year before, who became emaciated and suffered an appendicitis, complicated by peritonitis. A surgeon from Paris opened her stomach, and found so serious an abscess that after a few stitches the patient was given a day or two to live at the most: 'Then I slipped under the bolster of the sick woman one of those little sachets containing leaves from the roses with which Sister Thérèse of the Child Jesus had caressed her crucifix.' After three days the doctors declared that she was out of danger.[37]

CURE OF SISTER ALOYSIA   Sister Abysia (see p. 145 above) 'only obtained strength and courage in her trial through the instrumentality of heavenly perfumes which revealed the mysterious presence of her whom she had invoked'. Thérèse appeared to her and said: 'You will be cured, I promise you'. A doctor and a Paris surgeon confirmed the 'supernatural character' of her sudden cure.[38]

Protection of communities

Carmelite monasteries became special foci of devotion to Thérèse as her cause developed. The Carmel of Gallipoli, Italy, was the location of the most unusual of the many apparitions and miracles witnessed by nuns of the Order. On 25 February 1910 Reverend Mother Carmela of the Heart of Jesus, prioress at Gallipoli, wrote to Lisieux to describe a series of supernatural events thoroughly investigated by the bishop and reported to Rome.

At about three o'clock on 16 January 1909, kept awake by financial worries, the reverend mother fell asleep, and in a dream felt a hand touch her and cover her up tenderly. Thinking one of the Sisters had done this, she said: 'Leave me, for I am all in perspiration and the movement that you are making gives me too much air.' An unknown voice replied: 'No it, is a good act that I am doing,' and: 'Listen: Almighty God makes use of the inhabitants of heaven, as well as of those on earth, to assist his servants. Here are 500 francs, with which you will pay the debt of your community.' She pointed out that the debt was only 300 francs and was told: 'Well, the rest will be over and above. But since you may not keep this money in your cell, come with me.' The apparition added: 'Bilocation will help us.' Mother Carmela found herself led from her cell by a young Carmelite nun, 'whose habit and veil shone with a brightness of Paradise, which served to light us on our way', to the wooden accounts box, where she placed the 500 francs.

The prioress wrote again, in September 1910, that in the first four months of the year they had discovered surpluses inexplicable 'unless on the supposition that Sister Thérèse had slipped [them] into our cash box'. In May she saw 'little Thérèse again', and received further miraculous notes. In July she wished the prioress a happy feast and gave her a 5-lire note: 'But I did not accept it, and then she placed it at the foot of the little statue of the Sacred Heart . . . in our cell.'

The bishop told the Sisters that he had lost a 100-franc note when drawing up his accounts. He hoped Sister Thérèse would restore it. On 6 August Thérèse gave Mother Carmela a 100-franc banknote, which she sent to the bishop, who returned it to the community. She appeared to the prioress again, (her garments glittering 'with a light as of a transparent silver', her words with 'a melody as of an angel') on 5 September, the eve of the exhumation of her body, and said that 'only her bones' would be found, but they would 'work startling miracles and be powerful weapons against the devil'.

Bishop de Teil, Vice-Postulator of the cause, visited the Gallipoli Carmel and was told of an equally miraculous event on 6 January 1911, the anniversary of the first apparition, which was witnessed by the Bishop of Nardo. The bishop celebrated the anniversary by giving the Carmel the same sum of 500 francs, which he put in an envelope with a visiting card bearing the words: 'In Memoriam: MY WAY IS SURE; I AM NOT MISTAKEN. Sister Thérèse of the Child Jesus to Sister Maria-Carmela at Gallipoli; 16 January 1910. Pray for me daily that God may have mercy on me.' He inserted the envelope in a larger one sealed with his crest and inscribed, 'To be placed in the money-box and to be opened by Mother Prioress on 16 January 1911,' which he sent to the Carmel. He was to preach there on 16 January. The bishop knew that the nuns wanted to decorate the convent chapel, but this would cost 300 francs.

In January the prioress showed him his letter, still intact and in the box. He asked her to open it. She did so and handed it to him, saying: 'My Lord, take what belongs to you.' He was surprised to find 30 lire in addition to his envelope. He took his own note of 500 francs from the envelope, counted the notes for 300 francs, noticed that one emitted a perfume of roses, and replaced this with another. The envelope was intact. He decided that Thérèse wished to confirm the spiritual sense of the words: 'My way is sure'.

A strict inquiry by Bishop Muller of Gallipoli found that Sister Thérèse 'had procured for the Carmel of Gallipoli . . . important help, the source of which is unknown; she has thus drawn it from the distress and misery to which it had been reduced . . . These are undeniable facts.'[39]

Cures with a simultaneous apparition of Thérèse
On 12 April 1913, Michael McNelis, JP, of Donegal, Ireland, reported that on 24 January his wife had succumbed to puerperal fever after childbirth. On the morning of the 27th, three doctors diagnosed incurable septicaemia and were sure she was dying. A novena was made to the Little Flower, and more than once they said: ' "She is so busy, I wonder if she will think of poor Donegal!" Evidently she did think of it, and she "came down", as she promised to do, and comforted us all,' for at about eleven o'clock their four-year-old daughter, who had promised to make her first Communion in honour of Sister Thérèse if her mother was cured, brought a bunch of snowdrops into the house. She said a nun had told her to take

them 'to father for Mama, and Mama would be cured'. The flowers were put in water and after a time the whole house was 'filled with a strange, sweet perfume', even though snow-drops have no scent. When questioned, the child said that the nun, dressed in white, 'came down from the skies, put the flowers in her hand and . . . flew away' after delivering her message, although there were no nuns in the neighbourhood, and no snowdrops. 'My wife recovered promptly. . . . The flowers retained their wonderful scent for the space of a week.'[40]

SIGHT RESTORED   Theresa Neumann, a peasant girl from Konnersreuth, Bavaria, became famous as the stigmatic whose cult was suppressed during the Third Reich, mainly because she was born in Austria near the birthplace of Adolf Hitler. She was said neither to have eaten nor drunk for several years. Her visions of Christ's Passion were so intense that she experienced stigmata on hands and feet and bleeding from areas corresponding to Christ's wounds. As a young girl she was thought to be stupid and cumbersome. She became blind by accident when nineteen, took to her bed, unable to move apart from violent fits, and was pronounced incurable. She was deeply devoted to Thérèse, to whom she ascribed several cures of infirmities, such as the restoration of a twisted leg and the recovery of her ability to walk, but especially when, after starting a novena to Thérèse, she woke up blind as usual but felt someone touching her pillow. She looked up and saw her own hands and Thérèse's image on the wall. Her sight then improved rapidly and she entered the visionary period of her life.[41]

Cures evoked by a relic of Thérèse
CURE OF A TRAPPIST   On 27 June 1909, Abbot Marie Havur of Fontfroide, a refugee in Spain with his community,

described how in September 1908 lay brother Mary-Paul
noticed the symptoms of what became a painful stomach illness, probably cancer, and tolerable only with morphia injections. On 3 May the head of the infirmary advised: 'Since
human means are powerless to help you, make a novena of
prayers to Sister Thérèse.' The patient had read a summary of
Thérèse's life and had her photograph. On 4 May he was
exhausted, yet wanted to help the other brothers in their
work. He requested a relic of Sister Thérèse and put particles
of it in a drink, then waited. There were no more cruel pains;
the disease had disappeared. He went for a long walk, climbed
the nearby plateau without fatigue, returned and 'ate a hearty
meal of eggs, fried potatoes, raisins, nuts, and dried figs, finish-
ing with a good glass of wine, the first for eight months'. His
doctor signed an attestation.[42]

Cures and protection of soldiers during World War I
During the First World War the French civil and military
population experienced suffering and death on a hitherto
unknown scale. The national humiliation of the Franco-
Prussian war appeared minimal compared with the mass
slaughter and maiming, and destruction of families, property
and land, between 1914 and 1918. France was a war zone
where people were affected more acutely and lastingly than,
say, the British or Americans.

Initially, in 1914, there was a return to formal religious
practice (some commentators have called it an 'explosion of
religiousness'),[43] but from 1915 this public enthusiasm sub-
sided as the extent of sudden death and invalidity increased.
By 1917 most soldiers had returned to their condition at the
start of the conflict, 'religious or irreligious, moral or
immoral'.[44]

The French clergy were not exempt from military service,
and 32,699 priests, religious and seminarians were called up to

fight. About 1,300 were allowed to serve as stretcher-bearers and nurses. Since there were only 1,500 chaplains in the armed forces, the war led to an unprecedented two-way sharing of experience between the priests in the ranks and the often secularized masses with whom they served. The influence of these priests amidst the anguish and tragedy of trench life should not be underestimated when considering such religious phenomena as the many letters in the Catholic press ascribing escapes from death to the wearing of medals, scapulars, and images of the Sacred Heart and of saints. Prominent among the latter were the traditional 'protectors' of France: Blessed Joan of Arc (canonized in 1920 largely as a result of the war), St Geneviève, St Martin, St Rémi, but also Thérèse, who evoked an extraordinary devotion during the war, on both sides. In France at least one gun battery called itself the 'Batterie Soeur Thérèse', and, like several airmen, the flying ace Bourjade had her name and portrait painted on his machine. Illustrated books, such as *Histoire de l'Avion Soeur Thérèse* (The story of the Sister Thérèse Aeroplane), were devoted to her saving exploits. More than a million medals of Sister Thérèse were issued in 1915, largely because of the demand from the forces and their relatives. Tens of thousands of statues of Thérèse with roses were manufactured not only for churches but for the homes of combatants. In the same year the Carmel of Lisieux received five hundred letters a day from the front. The *Story of a Soul* became a leading spiritual text in France. Its popularity increased in Germany and Austria, too, where the future saint was invoked by men under arms as 'Schwester Thérèse', whereas the cult of Joan of Arc – undeniably a French nationalist and warrior saint – vanished there. After the war the Carmelites published a volume of extracts from the immense number of testimonies received from the Allied armed forces. The front cover shows Thérèse on a battlefield raising her hands over living, wounded and dead soldiers and a field-gun inscribed 'Sister Thérèse's Battery'. One soldier lies amidst the carnage reading *Story of a Soul*. A rain of roses falls from heaven over the scene and on a cathedral in flames in the background.[45]

CURE BY A RELIC   On 15 December 1914 Madame Marie Labitte wrote to Lisieux from Paris to describe a miracle worked for her son Robert by 'the lovable little Sister Thérèse'. On 14 October, a bullet had shattered his fibula and he was sinking fast because of infected blood and constant haemorrhages. He was given the last rites, kept alive only with ether and rum injections and by not changing the bandages, and expected to survive for forty-eight hours at the most. She placed a relic of Sister Thérèse under his pillow. That night, he became less restless, and slept. The next morning the doctor probed the wounds. To his amazement there was no haemorrhage. The leg, which had been swollen, discoloured, and a mass of septic wounds the day before had resumed its normal shape. The boy recovered his strength and the surgeon said it must be a miracle. 'Sister Thérèse had . . . done her self-appointed task. . . . Glory be to God! And honour to his faithful Spouse, Thérèse of the Child Jesus!'[46]

ESCAPE FROM DEATH   On 30 April 1915, René Demetière of the Third Zouaves, B Company, wrote from Dunkirk to describe his preservation 'through the intercession of dear Sister Thérèse'. The Germans bombarded the port with an enormous siege-gun. The writer fled from the quay to his hut, holding 'tightly in my hand a medal of Sister Thérèse'. He felt himself guided past the hut. He heard an explosion, threw himself on the ground, and was untouched by a sudden shower of stone, rails, and iron. The soldiers by the hut were killed outright or wounded. 'I love Sister Thérèse dearly, as a son loves a mother, and I feel entirely safe with her to shield me.'[47]

PROTECTION BY THE NURSE COMMANDANT   On 9 June 1915, Constant Beaudeau at the Volunteer Hospital of Vinça, Eastern Pyrenees, reported that on 5 March of that year a piece of shrapnel from a bursting bomb had become embedded in his right thigh. The surgeons did not try to extract it because the sciatic nerve was endangered. One of the nurses attached a relic of Sister Thérèse to the dressing. The next day the piece of metal had left the wound by itself. 'In my gratitude to the Little Saint, I do not forget to decorate her statue with flowers.' The nurse confirmed this 'new favour from Sister Thérèse of the Child Jesus – our "Nurse Commandant",' and enclosed the bomb splinter.[48]

PROTECTION FROM SHRAPNEL   On 25 May 1917, Sergeant Bosquet of the 70th Infantry wrote to Carmel 'from the armies at the Front . . . in the hope of obtaining greater glory for Sister Thérèse'. On 30 April his Company was decimated by machine guns when attacking the German lines. Sergeant Bosquet appealed to his friend and protectress: 'My little Sister, we have got to get out of this; it is up to you to find a way; find it, and I will let all the world know how you did it!' He was sent to take an order, went only a few steps and heard a tremendous crash behind him but felt no pain and went on. When night fell, he opened his haversack and saw his linen in rags, tins of sardines shattered, and papers in ashes. A piece of shrapnel had struck him in the back but had not penetrated his greatcoat. 'I knew then that I owed my life to my heavenly Protectress. I have now placed my men in her keeping.'[49]

Reconversions of members of the armed forces
Members of the armed forces often credited Thérèse with the restoration of their faith.

THE 'LITTLE UPHOLSTERER'   On 3 February 1918, in the last year of the war, 'G. D.' wrote from the Front to say that he had jettisoned Christianity as a young man. He was taken prisoner during the retreat from the Marne. A few days before, he had caught sight of a picture of Sister Thérèse in a book someone was reading, was strangely attracted by her 'seraphic countenance', and reconciled to God. When exchanged, through the Red Cross, he read the life of his 'heavenly benefactress': 'We soldiers . . . have our little pains each day, our humiliations and contradictions, which, accepted "with our most gracious smile", are transformed into "little joys"! . . . My God . . . you have sent your "little upholsterer" who has put everything right that I may receive you.' He learned later that his sister had sewn a relic of the 'Little Saint' into his uniform before he left for the Front.[50]

Various favours

The archives contain a vast number of reports of roses granted by Thérèse in the most varied situations. They include the extinguishing of a hotel ablaze and of a threatened forest fire on 1 August 1911 at Les Voirons, France, when there were only a few jugs of water to fight it: 'I threw into the flames a picture of Sister Thérèse, with a little piece of her clothing attached to it. Instantly the fir tree stopped burning of itself, and the sparks . . . ceased falling.'[51]

In June 1911 a New Forest pony with double pneumonia, though attended all night by groom and veterinary surgeon, was pronounced a hopeless case, which they wished to put out of its misery. Within a few minutes of his child owners saying 'Hail Marys to the Little Flower', he was walking, eating and drinking.[52]

In January 1912 a Dublin parish priest confirmed Thérèse's miraculous placing of a sovereign in a locked drawer for a poor family with only half-a-crown for food, unable to afford a first Communion suit and therefore subject to unutterable shame, far worse than that experienced nowadays by a child with the wrong brand name on trainers, clothes, or lunchbox food. The mother had merely sensed that the 'Little Flower was not far away', and said to herself: 'A sovereign would be enough!'[53]

At Recanati, an Italian fishing village on the verge of starvation because of inadequate catches, Agatha put a picture of Thérèse in the pocket of her husband Lancelot, cook on one of the boats. Thérèse was asked specifically for a sturgeon – never found in those waters. The nets were filled as soon as they were let down, and the catch included a magnificent sturgeon of more than a hundred pounds. Other boats caught nothing. There was a constant demand thereafter for pictures of the 'Santina'.[54]

★ ★ ★

On 10 July 1897, the dying Thérèse heard those round her discussing how death often contracts people's expressions in their last moments. She commented: 'Don't be upset if that happens to me, for immediately afterwards my face will be all smiles, for ever!'[55]

The Thérèse to whom so many millions of people have responded as to a living person is Thérèse the smiling flower in God's garden. She does not speak to them in consistent dogmatic statements but, like the great mystics, conveys her religious experiences through intuitions, images, symbols and metaphors. Unlike those of many mystics, however, Thérèse's insights are presented with a simplicity and assurance that make them directly meaningful for a wide variety of people. They sense her presence as that of a sympathetic, feeling individual who has suffered and endured as they have, and will help them to come through as she has done. In such moments theological niceties and metaphorical inconsistencies are banished and forgotten. Whether they are flowers in the garden now, or will be flowers in paradise; whether she is a flower or a strewer of flowers; whether Jesus lets the roses fall or lets Thérèse do so: none of this matters. The experience conveyed through the felt imagery is that roses can and do fall.

There is a mysterious space where our mundane desires to achieve and succeed, to survive poverty, war, decay, pain and sickness, to recover childlike purity, ardency and integrity, and escape failing enthusiasm or encroaching dryness of spirit, intermingle with a longing for ultimate purpose. It is in this space that so many people's hopes and wishes have focused, and continue to focus, on Thérèse. Her message, that 'Jesus asked us not only to love our neighbours as ourselves, but to love them as he loves them, and will love them until the end of time,' reaches people not so much through such straightforward statements as through the unfolding complex of images, anecdotes and everyday events united by her unique personality. Those who respond to Thérèse feel that her story is not limited by her birth and death, but is a continuing narrative in which their common human pains and needs and identification with her make her an ever-present, ever-sympathetic intercessor and immediate helper. The sources of her imagery, religious or secular, were not original and often disparate. But the way in which she combined them was unique; it was her own life. As she drew them together into her conviction of purpose, she preserved yet reworked their time-honoured associations to fit her religious experience.

The little wild flower (but also, as she described herself, the fledgling that has not lost its down, tiny lamb, little bride, minute jewel and radiant lily), Thérèse grows and unfolds in her family yet loses her mother and leaves even that protective enclosure in the wilderness of the secular world. She voluntarily sheds her petals, rejecting as it were the advice of the ungodly: 'Let us crown ourselves with rosebuds before they wither' (Wis. 2:8), and is nourished and sustained by Jesus, Sun and divine Child Gardener. He cultivates and dresses her to a rigorous order and symmetry in his garden of Carmel, where she nevertheless suffers the varying weather of life, and finally perishes with the assurance of rebirth in the garden of the Holy Child. Yet, even then:

> When a gardener makes a bouquet, he always finds little gaps between the splendid flowers; to fill out these gaps and prettily round off the whole bouquet, he sticks moss in between. You see, that is what I will be in heaven: a little sprig of moss among the glorious flowers God has there.[56]

There she fully realizes herself as a reflection of the Holy Face, thus fulfilling her wish and hope on entering the Order: 'I thought I was listening to my own story, so close was the resemblance between the little flower and little Thérèse. . . . No doubt God . . . will not leave his Little Flower to fade here below.'[57]

Through her writings and accounts of others' reception of them, people have felt and will continue to feel the presence of the Thérèse who said: 'I can't make heaven a feast of rejoicing; I can't rest as long as there are souls to be saved.' For them she will remain an active expression of the mystery at the heart of things until the moment when 'the angel will have said: "Time is no more!"; then I will take my rest. I'll be able to rejoice, because the number of the elect will be complete and because all will have entered into joy and repose. My heart beats with joy at this thought.'[58]

Abbreviations

DE	*Derniers Entretiens* (Paris, 1971)
DLTH	Descouvemont, Pierre and Loose, Helmuth Nils, *Thérèse et Lisieux* (Paris, 1991)
G	Giloteaux, Abbé Paulin, *Saint Teresa of the Child Jesus: her supernatural character*, tr. William Reany, STL (London, 1928)
GMC	Gouley, B., Mauger, R. and Chevalier, E., *Thérèse de Lisieux ou La Grande Saga d'une Petite Soeur 1897–1997* (Paris, 1997)
LC	Letters to Thérèse as in Letters (C I and II)
Letters (C I)	*Letters of St Thérèse of Lisieux*, tr. John Clarke, OCD, Vol. I, 1887–1890 (Washington, DC, 1982) (volume I of *Sainte Thérèse of Lisieux, General Correspondence*)
Letters (C II)	*Letters of St Thérèse of Lisieux*, tr. John Clarke, OCD, Vol. II, 1890–1897 (Washington, DC, 1982) (volume II of *Sainte Thérèse of Lisieux, General Correspondence*)
LD	Various letters between Thérèse's correspondents as in Letters (C I and II)
Letters (S)	*Collected Letters of Saint Thérèse de Lisieux, 1873–1897*, ed. Abbé Combes, tr. F. J. Sheed (London, 1949)
LT	Letters from Thérèse as numbered in OC

Ms A	Autobiographical manuscript dedicated to Mother Agnes of Jesus, 1895
Ms B	Autobiographical manuscript, letter to Sister Marie of the Sacred Heart, 1896
Ms C	Autobiographical manuscript dedicated to Mother Marie de Gonzague, 1897
NV	Last conversations of Thérèse as in *Novissima Verba* (Lisieux, 1927) and referred to thus in OC
OC	Thérèse de l'Enfant Jésus et de la Sainte-Face, *Œuvres complètes (Textes et Dernières Paroles)* (Paris, 2001)
OM	O'Mahony, Christopher, ed. and tr., *St Thérèse of Lisieux by those who knew her: Testimonies from the process of beatification* (Dublin, 1975)
Poems (E)	*Poems of Sr Teresa, Carmelite of Lisieux*, tr. Susan L. Emery (London & Boston, 1907–8)
PN	Individual poems as numbered in OC
RP	Thérèse's 'Pious Recreations' (plays and dramatic sketches) as numbered in OC and in *Récréations Pieuses et Prières* (Paris, 1992)
Pri	Thérèse's prayers as numbered in OC
SS (K)	*Thérèse of Lisieux, Autobiography of a Saint*, tr. Ronald Knox (London, 1958)
T	Teil, Roger de Basevi, *The Cause of Beatification of the Little Flower of Jesus* (London, 1913)
TNT (1912)	*A Little White Flower: The Story of Saint Thérèse of Lisieux*, tr. Thomas N. Taylor (London, 1912)
TNT (1926)	*A Little White Flower: The Story of Saint Thérèse of Lisieux* (revised), ed. and tr. T. N. Taylor (London, 1926)
TNT (1947)	*Saint Thérèse of Lisieux*, ed. and tr. T. N. Taylor (London, 1947)

Notes

Introduction

1. 'Les Anges à la Crèche de Jésus', author's translation. Cf., RP2 1v, 25 December 1894, OC, p. 801; *Histoire d'une Âme* (Lisieux, 1898); Poems (E), p. 104; *Poems of St. Thérèse of the Child Jesus*, tr. Carmelites of Santa Clara (London, 1925). Thérèse uses the flower symbol fifteen times in this piece. The identification of flowers with souls is even more explicit when she writes more metaphorically, as in the prologue to Manuscript A of her autobiography: 'And so it is in the world of souls, Jesus' garden.' (Ms A, 2v). Although the repetition of a key term such as 'flowers' can have a discordant effect in English, it does not necessarily jar in French (and in German, and so on) where the vocabulary available to the writer is comparatively restricted.

2. We know this from the notes taken by Sister Marie of St Joseph (a Sister who had lost her mother at the age of nine, and whom Thérèse had befriended. Sister Marie was prone to fits of depression and was all but ostracized by the other nuns). See Letters (C II), pp. 905, 988.

3. '. . . déformations imbéciles et toutes les roses en patisserie', François Mauriac, quoted in *Fêtes et Saisons. Sainte Thérèse de Lisieux*, No. 509 (November, 1996), p. 7. See François Mauriac, *Bloc-Notes*, Vols. 1–5 (Paris, 1958–71) and *Nouveaux Mémoires Intérieurs* (Paris, 1965), *passim*, for discussions of St Thérèse and his own understanding of the 'little way'.

4. Of, indeed, 'une robuste petite Normande . . .': 'a robust little Norman girl, firmly attached to the real world and to life, with her feet on the real earth, and evidently well aware of what she wants to do'. Maxence van der Meersch, *La Petite Sainte Thérèse* (Paris, 1947), p. 250.

5. This has been recommended, explicitly or implicitly, by some commentaries which, often for the best purposes, have sought to remove the 'real Thérèse' from her showers of roses, either by detaching her from the language and practice which they have decried as the outdated conventual practice of the nineteenth century, or by setting her in or against a reconstructed social or ideological context. Thus van der Meersch remarks: 'The environment in which St Thérèse lived is only

too accurately betrayed by the tone of her verse – "fiancée of Christ . . . dying from love . . . azure wings . . . virginal flames". All this does not diminish the real merits of her writings but irritatingly recalls the sickening sentimentality that alienates so many well-intentioned people from the practice of religion.' (van der Meersch, *La Petite Sainte Thérèse*, p. 246).

6. The novelist Georges Bernanos during an interview in Brazil in 1939, quoted in Robert Speaight, *Georges Bernanos* (London, 1973), p. 266. This aspect was not wholly overlooked by the 'official' Church, for, on 17 May 1927, Pope Pius XI dedicated a statue of Thérèse in the Vatican gardens and appointed her the 'sacred keeper of gardens'; See GMC, p. 136, quoting Jean Vinatier, *Mère Agnès de Jésus* (Paris, n.d.). Accordingly, she is cited as patron of florists, gardeners and so on.

7. See *Histoire d'une Âme* (Lisieux, 1898); ibid., rev. edn (Lisieux, *c*.1915); OC, pp. 71–4; TNT (1926), pp. 4–7 (adapted).

8. OC, p. 73.

9. In a letter of 16 November 1896 to her aunt, Mme Guérin, she wrote: 'The poet who had the daring to say: "What is well thought is clearly uttered / And the words to say it come easily" certainly never felt what I feel in the depths of my heart!' (LT 202, OC, pp. 562–3; Letters (S), p. 262). The quotation, 'Ce que l'on conçoit bien s'énonce clairement / Et les mots pour le dire arrivent aisément,' is from Boileau's *L'Art poétique*, chant premier (cf. Boileau Despréaux, *Oeuvres* [Paris, 1822], p. 195). Although Sister Marie of the Trinity remarked in a letter of 1932 to Mother Agnes that Thérèse did not learn the rules of versification and refused to look at a treatise on versification proffered to her by Marie, this is less than the truth, and, like the citation, merely shows that Thérèse wished to stress her conviction that the inspiration of the heart was more important than exact measure in poetry. She was aware of the main lines of Boileau's recommendations as far as they were relevant to the 'outpouring' of her heart, but did not bother with the detailed niceties of his entire work on composition. See n.1, Letters (C II), p. 1022.

10. See OC, pp. 628, 1257; Jean-François Six, *La véritable enfance de Thérèse de Lisieux: Névrose et sainteté* (Paris, 1972), p. 176.

11. Among her last words to Céline she quoted some lines from Hugo's poem on Louis XVII, which clearly recalled an occasion when her father had recited them as a lullaby: 'Soon you will come with me / . . . and cradle the crying child / And breathe out such luminosity as will renew suns in their fiery domain . . .' ('Vous viendrez bientôt avec moi / . . . bercer l'enfant qui pleure / Et, dans leur brûlante demeure / D'un souffle lumineux rajeunir les soleils . . .'), 'Dernières Paroles de Thérèse à Céline, Juillet-Septembre 1897', OC, p. 1152.

12. 'Naître avec le printemps, mourir avec les roses', 'Le Papillon', in Alphonse-Louis-Marie de Lamartine, *Premières et Nouvelles Méditations Poétiques* (Paris, 1855), p. 198.

13. 'Sur le chemin de nos douleurs / Tu sèmes le sol d'espérances, / Comme on borde un linceul de fleurs!', 'Les Fleurs', Lamartine, *Premières et Nouvelles Méditations Poétiques*, p. 140.

14. 'Cueillons, cueillons la rose au matin de la vie', 'Elégie', ibid., p. 201.

15. 'Voilà pourquoi les fleurs, ces prières écloses / Dont Dieu lui-même emplit les corolles de miel, / Pures comme ces lis, chastes comme ces roses, / Semblent prier pour nous dans ces maisons du ciel.' 'Les Fleurs sur l'Autel', ibid., p. 292.

16. 'Le temps est ton navire et non pas ta demeure', 'Réflexion', ibid., p. 337.

17. 'Je vis un ange blanc qui passait sur ma tête; / . . . Es-tu la mort? lui dis-je, ou bien es-tu la vie? . . . / Et l'ange devint noir, et dit: – Je suis l'amour', 'L'Apparition', Victor Hugo, *Les Contemplations* (Paris, 1965), p. 335.

18. '. . . Dieu bénit l'homme, / Non pour avoir trouvé, mais pour avoir cherché', 'La Vie aux Champs', ibid., pp. 27–8.

19. 'Unité', ibid., p. 72; author's translation.

20. 'La Marguerite', 'Ces Roses du Bengale', author's translation; cf. Rose Harel, *L'Alouette aux Blés* (Préface par Adolphe Bordes), 2nd edn (Lisieux, 1864); Marie de Besneray, *Assises littéraires de 'la Pomme'. Rose Harel, servante-poète* (Caen, 1902), pp. 10–12. See also Jacques Viquesnel, *Promenades en Normandie avec Sainte Thérèse de Lisieux* (Condée-sur-Noireau, 1993), p. 142.

21. 'Céline's Canticle' ('Le Cantique de Céline'), author's translation; cf. Poems (E); OC, pp. 671–75.

22. Aquilas Chaudé, *La Théologie des Plantes* (Paris, 1882), pp. 107, 247–8, 250.

23. Also known in English as 'The Beauties of Christianity', it was published the day before the ceremony in the Cathedral of Notre Dame solemnly attended by Napoleon Bonaparte and held to commemorate the restoration of Catholicism as the state religion of France, and seemed to mark not merely Chateaubriand's own recovery of belief but the regeneration of France as one of the foremost inheritors and defenders of a European civilization produced by Christianity, the demonstrably true faith. It was translated into many languages and remained a resource book of Catholics all over the world long after Bonapartism was dead.

24. Ronald Knox, in the preface to Thomas à Kempis, *The Imitation of Christ*, tr. R. Knox and M. Oakley (London, 1959), p. 6, from which the following passage (with adaptations) is taken.

25. Thomas à Kempis, ibid., pp. 104–5, 137 (adapted).

26. Ms A 83r; TNT (1926), p.172; OC, p. 210.

27. *The Complete Works of St John of the Cross*, tr. and ed. E. Allison Peers (London, 1964), Vol. II: 'Spiritual Songs Between the Soul and the Spouse', p. 275 (adapted); pp. 180–1 (commentary, pp. 269–76; esp.:

'The flowers as we have said, are the virtues of the soul. The rose trees are the faculties of the same soul: memory, understanding and will; these bear and nurture flowers of Divine conceptions and acts of love and of the said virtues.') Cited by Thérèse in French in a letter to Céline of 15 August 1892: LT 135; Letters (S), p. 152; OC, p. 448.

28. *Positio super introductione Causae Bajocensis sue Lexoviensis Beatificationis et Canonizationis Servae Dei Sor. Theresiae* . . . (Rome, 1914), vol. xx, p. 82; Stéphane-Joseph Piat, *Léonie: Une soeur de Sainte Thérèse à la Visitation* (Lisieux, 1966), pp. 126–7.

29. François de Sales, *Introduction à la Vie Dévote* (1605; 5th edn 1619). See St Francis de Sales, *Introduction to the Devout Life*, tr. Alan Ross (London, 1924), p. xxiii (adapted).

30. Ibid., pp. 63–4.

31. Charles Arminjon, *Fin du monde présent et mystères de la vie future* (n.p., 1881; Lisieux, 1970), pp. 11, 131–2, 134–6, 270.

32. See, e.g. DE, [26] September 1897; OC, p. 1162.

33. OC, pp. 1237–8; cf. *Bienheureux Théophane Vénard. Lettres choisies*, ed. Jean Guennou (Paris, 1960).

34. DLTH, p. 269.

Chapter 1

1. She wrote: ' "God", says the author of the *Imitation*, "communicates himself sometimes amid great light, at other times sweetly veiled under signs and figures".' (TNT [1926], p. 92; *Imitation of Christ*, III, 43.4). See also DE 21–6 (May 1897); OC, p. 1001.

2. OM, p. 208.

3. Ms A 2v; OC, p. 72.

4. Ms A 83r; OC, p. 210.

5. LC 9; OC, p. 1013. On 9 June 1897, Sister Marie of the Sacred Heart told Thérèse that they would be very sad after she died. Thérèse replied: 'Oh! No, you will see . . . it will be like a shower of roses.' She added: 'After my death, you will go to the letter box, and you will find many consolations' (DE 1: 438; OC, p. 1176).

6. In her testimony, Marie recalled Thérèse's words: 'We must treasure the rose petals', which she had placed one by one round her crucifix; as the petals slipped from her bed to the floor, she said to the Sisters: 'Collect them carefully. Don't miss one of them. You will find them a source of joy later.' DE, 14 September 1897; OC, p. 1128. See also OM, p. 103.

7. See DLTH, p. 315.

8. See GMC, p. 233.

9. 'Des Roses', author's translation. Cf. Poems (E), p. 95; RP 5 (6), OC, pp. 876–7.

10. See OC, pp. 439–40, 1099, 1425.

11. Walter de la Mare, *Complete Poems* (London, 1969), p. 116.

12. Ms A 79v; OC, p. 204.
13. Ms B 3v; OC, p. 226.
14. Dante Alighieri, *The Vision of Purgatory and Paradise*, tr. H. F. Cary (London, 1893), Canto XXXI (100–27), p. 436 (see also Canto XXX [124–7], Canto XXXI [4–22]).
15. See M. C. Ghyka, *Le nombre d'or*, vol. 2 (Paris, 1931), p. 41; Ann Mayhew, *The Rose: Myth, Folklore and Legend* (London, 1979), p. 75; DLTH, pp. 318–19.
16. The series of psychological setbacks suffered by Thérèse affected her deeply. When her sister Pauline entered the convent, Thérèse felt she had lost a 'second mother'. She was profoundly distressed when unable to make her first Communion together with her class, because she had been born just two days too late to allow her to do so in 1883. From December to Easter she was often ill, and on Easter Saturday was attacked by fits of trembling, which lasted for six weeks. Dr Gayral described this illness as a 'neurotic crisis resulting from frustration' (OC, p. 1252, n. 94).
17. It was a gift to Louis Martin when still a bachelor from Mlle Felicité Baudouin, who had helped him to start his watch-making and jewellery shop in the rue du Pont Neuf. Louis placed the statue at the end of a central alley in a property he had bought close to his shop, and used as a retreat. After his marriage in 1858, the statue entered the family home and became the focus of their evening prayers, and sometimes of special petitions for conversions and healing. In 1870 Mme Martin, upset by the death of her five-year-old daughter, Hélène, found consolation before the statue when an inner voice said: 'She is here, beside me.' When her older daughters said they wanted to pray before a less imposing figure, she told them she had been granted so many graces before it that it would never leave the house as long as she lived. It is now in a niche above Thérèse's shrine in Lisieux.
18. DE, 21 August 1897; LC, p. 161; OC, p. 1103. See also Ms A 30r, OC, p. 116; Ms A 2r, OC, p. 71; Pri I, May 1883, OC, p. 957; Pri 21, OC, p. 976.
19. 'Why I Love You, O Mary' (PN 54; OC, p. 750) which, on 21 August, she told Pauline included everything she had wanted to preach about Our Lady (DE; OC, p. 1104).
20. TNT (1947), p. 112; OC, pp. 172–3. See also Ms A 61r–61v; OC, pp. 172–3; TNT (1926), pp. 121–2; Ms A 85v; OC, p. 215.
21. 'Sainte Cécile', Poems (E), pp. 62–3 (adapted); OC, pp. 638–40.
22. Letter to Pauline, 4 (?) July 1881, OC, p. 301; Letters (S), p. 9.
23. '*The Little Flowers' and the Life of St Francis with the 'Mirror of Perfection'*, tr. T. Okey, R. Steele and E. Gurney Salter (London, 1910), p. 293.
24. Ms B 3r, OC, p. 224.
25. See Letters (S), p. 268; LT 213, OC, p. 570.
26. *Cantico di fratre Sole* (Song of Brother Sun). See Okey et al. (eds), '*The Little Flowers*', p. 295.

27. OC, p. 1022.
28. Letters (S), p. 88; LT 89, OC, p. 389. See also OC, pp. 1233–4.
29. St Francis de Sales, *Introduction to the Devout Life*, tr. A. Ross (London, 1924), pp xxiii, 63–4. (See Introduction, pp. 20–1 above.)
30. Ibid., pp. 77–8.
31. See Anne Winston-Allen, *Stories of the Rose: the making of the rosary in the Middle Ages* (Pennsylvania, 1997), pp. 88, 100–1; John D. Miller, *Beads and Prayers: The Rosary in History and Devotion* (London, 2001), p. 3.
32. Ms C 25v; OC, pp. 268–9. See also DE, 20 August; OC, p. 1102.
33. S. J. Piat, *Léonie* (Lisieux, 1966), p. 149.
34. J. G. Frazer, *The Golden Bough: A study in magic and religion*, Vol. I: *The Magic Art* (London, 1935), pp. 87–109; Mircea Eliade, *Traité d'histoire des réligions*, 2nd edn (Paris, 1965), p. 230 and *passim*.
35. Later, in June 1897, she wrote on a scrap of paper: 'My God, with the help of your grace I am ready to spill all my blood.' DLTH, pp. 259, 261.
36. Ms C 4v–5r; OC, p. 240.
37. Even though Pauline recorded her saying that she was not just fond of flowers and roses but of red flowers and beautiful pink daisies. See DE 7 (28 August 1897); OC, p. 1115.
38. Ms A 72v; OC, p. 192. She stresses the word 'snow' by writing it in capitals and follows it with an exclamation mark.
39. See LT 105, 10 May 1890; Letters (S), p. 109; OC, p. 409. See also LT 124, 20 October 1890, Letters (S), p. 135; OC, p. 433.
40. Not only because 'anaemia was an almost invariable clinical feature, but also because of its long association with childhood, innocence and even holiness'; Thomas Dormandy, *The White Death: A History of Tuberculosis* (New York, 2000), p. xiv.
41. See the photograph reproduced in DLTH, p. 318.
42. See Mayhew, *The Rose*, pp. 39–42.
43. See, e.g., Patricia Davis, *Aromatherapy: an A–Z* (Saffron Walden, 1988), pp. 289–91.
44. *Selections from the Writings of John Ruskin* (London, 1862), p. 309.
45. Ibid., pp. 74–5 (cf. John Ruskin, *Modern Painters*, Vol. 5 [London, 1860], pt. 6, ch. 10).
46. Ms A 29v; TNT (1926), p. 59; OC, p. 117.
47. 'Une Fleur,' RP 5 (14); Poems (E), p. 94 (adapted); OC, p. 880.
48. PN 18; OC, pp. 671–9.
49. LT 98, 22 October 1889; Letters (S), p. 102; OC, p. 398.
50. See OM, p. 96.
51. An occasion reminiscent of Hopkins' lament for the felling of 'Binsey Poplars': 'O if we but knew what we do / When we delve or hew . . . / Hack and rack the growing green!', *Poems of Gerard Manley Hopkins*, 4th edn, eds W. H. Gardner and N. H. Mackenzie (London, 1967), p. 78.
52. LT 134; Letters (S), p. 150; OC, p. 446.

53. LT 187; Letters (S), p. 234; OC, p. 536.
54. LT 240, 3 June 1897; Letters (S), p. 301; OC, p. 597.
55. 'Une couronne de Lys', RP 5 (18); Poems (E), p. 119 (adapted); OC, p. 882.
56. See the illustrations in DLTH, pp. 149, 207.
57. See DLTH, pp. 220–1.
58. LT 141, 25 April 1893; Letters (S), pp. 163–5; OC, p. 461.
59. Ibid.
60. LT 55, Letters (S), p. 91; OC, p. 348.
61. PN 35; Poems (E), p. 26 (adapted); OC, p. 719.
62. LT 55, 5–9 July 1888; Letters (S), p. 91; OC, p. 348.
63. Ms A 50v; OC, p. 152. See DLTH, p. 76 for an illustration of the dried flower Thérèse stuck on a picture of Our Lady of Victories.
64. Ms A 3v, 4r; OC, pp. 73–4.
65. Ms A 2v, TNT (1926), p. 5; OC, p. 72. See the 'Canticle of Céline' (PN 18; OC, p. 671) and the 'Last Conversations' (DE, OC, p. 1127) for similar references.
66. Lucie Delarue-Mardrus, *Sainte Thérèse of Lisieux: a biography*, tr. H. Y. Chase (London, 1929), pp. 114–15.
67. LT 135, 15 August 1892; Letters (S), p. 152; OC, p. 448.
68. DE, 4 August 1897; OC, p. 1076. See also the illustration in DLTH, p. 302.
69. LT 18; Letters (S), p. 14; OC, pp. 306, 1296 (n. 1).
70. Ms A 35v; OC, p. 126.
71. LT 124, 20 October 1890; Letters (S), pp. 135–6; OC, p. 433.
72. LT 132, 20 October 1891; Letters (S), p. 146; OC, p. 444.
73. LT 134, 26 April 1892; Letters (S), p. 150; OC, p. 447.
74. 'Jésus mon Bien-Aimé, rappelle-toi!', PN 24; Poems (E), p. 18, (adapted); OC, p. 698.
75. Ms A 13r; TNT (1926), p. 25; OC, p. 89.
76. LT 132; Letters (S), pp. 146–7; OC, p. 443, n. 2.
77. LT 141; Letters (S), pp. 163–5; OC, p. 461.
78. 'Divine Dew, or Mary's Virginal Milk', 'La Rosée Divine ou Le Lait Virginal de Marie', PN 1; Poems (E), p. 47 (adapted); OC, p. 635.
79. PN 24 (21); Poems (E), pp. 21–2 (adapted); OC, p. 697.
80. Ms A 46v; TNT (1926), p. 90; OC, p. 144.
81. Author's translation. See PN 44; OC, p. 732. See also RP 2 (4), OC, p. 813, where she describes the infant Jesus watering souls with the dew of baptism before transplanting them to his heavenly garden, and Ms C 2r, TNT (1926), p. 178, OC, p. 236, where she characterizes her remembered humiliations as 'precious dew-drops'.
82. LT 102; Letters (S), p. 107; OC, p. 406.
83. PN 2, 20 February 1894; OC, p. 637.
84. LT 169, 19 August 1894; Letters (S), p. 210; OC, p. 507.
85. PN 17; Poems (E) (adapted); OC, p. 667.

86. PN 20; Poems (E) (adapted); OC, p. 684.
87. Ms C 36v; TNT (1926), p. 240; OC, pp. 284–5.

Chapter 2

1. Gustave Flaubert, *Madame Bovary*, tr. E. Marx-Aveling (London, 1886), p. 39, epitomizing the attitudes of such stock figures of French Romanticism as Chateaubriand's René: 'The absolute solitude, the spectacle of nature, soon immersed me in a state almost beyond words. . . . I was overcome by a superabundance of life.' Cf. F. R. de Chateaubriand, *Oeuvres Choisies*, vol. II (Paris, 1912), p. 511.
2. S.-J. Piat, OFM, *The Story of A Family* (Dublin, 1947), p. 38.
3. Author's translation, and see ibid., p.108.
4. Soeur Geneviève [Céline], *Conseils et Souvenirs* (Paris, 1952), p. 87. See also Sister Geneviève of the Holy Face, *A Memoir of my Sister Saint Thérèse* (Dublin, 1959), p. 119.
5. See Jacques Maître, *L'Orpheline de la Bérésina* (Paris, 1995), p. 37.
6. Louise Swanton Belloc, *La Tirelire aux histoires: lectures choisies* (Paris, 1870), p. 4.
7. TNT (1947), p. 41; Ms A 11v; OC, pp. 85–6. See also, Céline's letter (10–17 June 1877) to Marie, on retreat at Le Mans, reporting that the six geraniums and the dahlias in their garden had grown longer than her finger.
8. TNT (1926), p. 41; Ms A 12r; OC, p. 87.
9. TNT (1926), p. 44; Ms A 13r; OC, p. 89.
10. TNT (1947), pp. 44–5; OC, p. 1249, n. 48.
11. See Marcel Proust, *À la Recherche du Temps Perdu*, Vol. II (Paris, 1954), pp. 70, 94–7, and *passim*. Thérèse wrote: 'Far-off sounds wafted towards me on the murmuring breeze, and faint notes of [military] music from the neighbouring town tinged my thoughts with gentle melancholy.' See TNT (1947), p. 46; Ms A 14v; OC, p. 91.
12. Jules Verne, 'Lisieux', in *Géographie Illustrée de la France et de ses Colonies* (Paris, n.d. [1870]), p. 119. Alençon, however, receives an accolade for its broad, clean streets and avenues of splendid chestnut trees (ibid., p. 493).
13. TNT (1947), p. 47; Ms A 14v–15r; OC, p. 92.
14. TNT (1947), pp. 45–6; Ms A 14r; OC, p. 91.
15. TNT (1947), pp. 379–81 (adapted); PN 18, OC, pp. 671–9.
16. See Letters (C I), pp. 131–5.
17. LD, 29 July 1885, Letters (C I), p. 228.
18. SS (K), p. 59; Ms A 22r; OC, pp. 103–4.
19. OM, p. 184.
20. TNT (1926), p. 50; Ms A 26v; OC, p. 110.
21. TNT (1926), pp. 47–8; Ms A 25v; OC, p. 109.
22. OM, p. 97.

23. LC 7 From Sister Agnes of Jesus to Thérèse, December 1882 or January 1883; see Letters (C I), p. 157.
24. Piat, *The Story of A Family*, p. 40.
25. TNT (1926), pp. 55–6; Ms A 29v; OC, pp. 115–16.
26. TNT (1926), pp. 57–9; Ms A 30r/v; OC, p. 117.
27. LC 12, 13, May 1883; see Letters (C I), pp. 170–1.
28. Letters from Pauline, ibid., pp. 150–80.
29. LT 9 from Thérèse to Mother Marie de Gonzague, November–December 1882(?); OC, p. 302; Letters (S), p. 10.
30. In 1909 this collection was published with some alterations as *Deux mois et neuf jours de preparation à ma première communion* ('Two Months and Nine Days of Preparation for my First Communion').
31. LT 11; OC p. 303; Letters (S), p.12. See also LC 20, Pauline to Thérèse, 7 February 1884, Letters (C I), p. 184.
32. TNT (1926), p. 65; Ms A 33r; OC, p. 121.
33. See Letters (C I), pp. 185, 191, nn. 3–4; see also the illustration of Thérèse's copybook in DLTH, p. 54.
34. See LC 23, 25, 26, 27, 29, 31; Pauline's letters to Thérèse of 28 February, 6, 13, 27 March, 10 April, 6 May 1884; Letters (C I), pp. 187 (n. 1), 188, 192, 193, 195, 197, 199.
35. TNT (1926) (adapted), p. 68; Ms A 35r; OC, pp. 124–5.
36. TNT (1926), pp. 61–2; Ms A 31v; OC, p. 119. See also the poem Céline gave to Thérèse when she made her first Communion (8 May 1884), text in Letters (C II), pp. 1277–9, illustrated in DLTH, p. 56.
37. Ms A 42v; OC, p. 138. See SS (K), pp. 96–7.
38. LT 21/LC 45, Pauline's letter to Céline and Thérèse of 22 or 24 October 1886; Letters (C I), p. 253.
39. LT 22/LC 49, Pauline's letter to Thérèse and Céline of 16 June 1887; Letters (C I), p. 271.
40. Ms A 46v; OC, p. 144.
41. TNT (1926), pp. 103–4; Ms A 53r; OC, p. 157. See also Piat, *The Story of A Family*, p. 282.
42. TNT (1926), p. 98; Ms A 50v; OC, p. 152.
43. Ibid.
44. LT 27 to Pauline; OC, p. 320; Letters (S), pp. 22–4.
45. LT 27/LC 56, Pauline to M. Guérin, 21 October 1887; Letters (C I), pp. 295–6.
46. TNT (1947), p. 97; Ms A 51v; OC, p. 154.
47. TNT (1947), pp. 106–7; Ms A 57–8v; OC, pp. 166–7.
48. TNT (1947), p. 107; Ms A 58v; OC, p. 168.
49. TNT (1947), p. 119; Ms A 67r; OC, p. 182.
50. Ms A 71r; OC, p. 189.
51. See Ms B 4r/v; OC, p. 228; Letters (C I), pp. 182–3.

Chapter 3

1. TNT (1926), p. 136 (adapted); Ms A 69v; OC, p. 186.
2. TNT (1926), p. 137; Ms A 69v; OC, p. 187.
3. *A Treatise on Charity*, ch. vi.
4. See TNT (1926), pp. 168–9; Ms A 81v; OC, pp. 207–8. See also Sister Geneviève, *A Memoir of my Sister Saint Thérèse* (Dublin, 1959), pp. 119–20.
5. Sister Geneviève, *Memoir*, pp. 129–30. Cf. DLTH, p.132.
6. LT 49, 12–30 May 1888; OC, p. 343; Letters (S), pp. 44–5.
7. LC 81, 20 May 1888; Letters (C I), p. 432.
8. LD, 7 June 1888; LD, 10 June 1888; Letters (C I), pp. 432–3.
9. See LC 104, 6–9 January 1889 (?); Letters (C I), p. 509.
10. LC 102, 7 January 1889; Letters (C I), p. 506.
11. See Ms A 72v; OC, p.192; TNT (1926), pp. 146–7.
12. 'The veil meant even more than mere self-control and modest restraint. Thérèse desired not only inconspicuousness but misunderstanding. She knew whom she was following . . . This was the finest flower of her devotion to the Holy Face. She overcame her pride, her desire for status – that most powerful of human impulses, which at times stabbed her young heart with fiery stings – by wearing the veil of the smile.' Ida Friederike Görres, *The Hidden Face: A Study of Thérèse of Lisieux*, tr. R. and C. Winston (London, 1959), p. 311.
13. LT 102, 27 April 1890; OC, pp. 405–6; Letters (S), p.106. Cf. LT 104, OC, p. 407; LT 105, OC, p. 408.
14. Letters (C I), p. 613 n. 5. Cf. LT 108; OC, p. 412; Letters (S), p. 115.
15. Letter to Pauline, April–May 1890, Letters (S), pp. 107–8. Cf. LT 103, 4 May (?) 1890; OC, p. 406; Letters (C I), pp. 612–13.
16. LT 57, 23 July 1888; OC, pp. 349–50; Letters (S), pp. 48–9. Cf. Letters (C I), pp. 450–1, notes; LT 83, February 1889; OC, pp. 381–2; Letters (S), p. 78.
17. LT 107, Thérèse to Céline, 19–20 May 1890; OC, p. 410; Letters (S), p.113.
18. LT 105, May 1890; OC, pp. 408–9; Letters (S), p. 109.
19. Ms A 76v–77r; OC, p. 199; TNT (1926), pp. 156–7 (adapted).
20. Ms A 84v; OC, p. 213; TNT (1926), p. 176.
21. See DLTH, p. 197.
22. Sister Geneviève, *Memoir*, op. cit., pp. 49–50.
23. LT 122, Thérèse to Céline, 14 October 1890; OC, p. 430; Letters (S), p. 133.
24. LT 123, Thérèse to Mme Guérin, 15 October 1890; OC, pp. 431–2; Letters (S), pp. 134–5.
25. LT 124, 20 October 1890; OC, p. 433; Letters (S), p. 136.
26. LT 130, 23 July 1891; OC, p. 440; Letters (S), p. 144.

27. Ms A 79r; OC, p. 203; TNT (1926), pp. 163–4.
28. LT 132, Thérèse to Céline, 20 October 1891; OC, pp. 443–4; Letters (S), pp. 146–7.
29. LT 134, Thérèse to Céline, 26 April 1892; OC, pp. 446–8; Letters (S), pp. 150–2.
30. LT 141, letter to Céline, 25 April 1893; OC, p. 461; Letters (S), pp. 163–5.
31. '. . . which is wont to rise and dissolve in the air', cf. the explanation of the Spiritual Canticle, stanza XXXI, *The Complete Works of St John of the Cross*, tr. and ed. E. Allison Peers (London, 1964), Vol. II, p. 339.
32. DE, 7 April; OC, p. 992.
33. See DLTH, p. 159.
34. LT 156; OC, p. 486; Letters (S), p. 189. See also LT 160 to Sister Marie-Aloysia Vallée, 3 April 1894; OC, p. 492; Letters (S), p. 194.
35. RP 2, 25 December 1894; OC, pp. 801–18. Cf. Letters (C II), p. 905, n. 2.
36. See OC, pp. 960–2; *The Prayers of Saint Thérèse of Lisieux*, tr. Alethia Kane, OCD (Washington, 1997), pp. 48–50.
37. LT 187, 30 April 1896; OC, p. 536; Letters (S), p. 234.
38. Ms B 4r/v; OC, p. 228; TNT (1926), pp. 255–6 (adapted).
39. PN 34 'Jeter les Fleurs', (28 June 1896); OC, pp. 717–8; 'To Scatter Flowers' tr. Susan L. Emery in TNT (1947), p. 383 (adapted).
40. LT 194; OC, p. 548; Letters (C II), pp. 989–90.
41. Is. 58.10 (AV).
42. See DE 21 to 26 May; OC, p. 1000.
43. LT 245; OC, p. 602; Letters (S), p. 305.
44. 'To Théophane Vénard, Priest of the Foreign Mission Society, martyred at Tonkin at the age of 31', Poems (E), p. 82 (adapted); 'À Théophane Vénard', PN 47, 2 February 1897; OC, p. 737.
45. 'My Joy', Poems (E), p. 36 (adapted); 'Ma Joie'; PN 45, 21 January 1897; OC, pp. 733–4.
46. Ibid.
47. LT 224, from Thérèse to Father Bellière, 25 April 1897 (in response to his letter, LC 177, 17 April 1897), OC, pp. 583–4; Letters (S), pp. 286–7.
48. According to Sister Marie of the Trinity. See OC, p. 1395.
49. 'A Rose without Petals', Poems (E), p. 42 (adapted); 'Une rose effeuillée', PN 51, 19 May 1897; OC, p. 744.
50. Sister Marie's testimony of 17 January 1935. See OC, pp. 1394–5. see also PN 54, v. 22, OC, p. 755.
51. TNT (1926), pp. 177–8 (adapted); Ms C 1r/1v/2r; OC, pp. 235–6.
52. LT 240, 3 June (?) 1897, from Thérèse to Sister Marie of the Trinity, OC, p. 597; Letters (S), p. 301.
53. DE, 7 June (2) 1897; OC, p. 1012.
54. DE, 11 June 1897; OC, p. 1176. See also OC, p. 1462, n. 20.
55. LT 246, from Thérèse to Sister Marie of the Trinity, 13 June 1897; OC, p. 602; Letters (S), p. 304.

56. DE, 25 July (8) 1897; OC, p. 1058.
57. DE, 5 August 1897 (7) (9); OC, p. 1079.
58. DE, 6 August 1897 (8); OC, pp. 1082–3.
59. DE 13, September 1897 (2); OC, p. 1127.
60. DE, 14 September 1897(1); OC, p. 1128.
61. DE; OC, p. 1190.
62. Ibid.
63. DE, 24 September 1897(4); OC, p. 1135.
64. OM, p. 127.
65. Ibid., pp. 161–2.

Chapter 4

1. 19 July 1897, OC, p. 1051.
2. LT 193, 30 July 1896; OC, pp. 547–8; Letters (S), p. 246.
3. Ms A 46v, OC, p. 144.
4. For Thérèse's comments on Aloysius see DE, 21 May 1897, in OC, p. 1000: 'I find Théophane Vénard much more pleasing than St Aloysius of Gonzaga because St Aloysius' life is extraordinary and Théophane's quite ordinary.'
5. OC, p. 1176.
6. See TNT (1927), p. 241. Sister Martha of Jesus remembered that she and Mother Marie-Ange had smelled a 'strong, sweet fragrance of heliotrope' near the statue in the oratory of the Child Jesus. In spite of initial doubts, Sister Martha smelled a 'strong scent of roses' coming from the oratory next door to her cell, felt a 'little puff of rose-scented wind' quite a long way from the cell, and had similar experiences 'about fifteen times' in the two years before her testimony for the cause. See OM, pp. 166–7, 228.
7. Quoted in GMC, p. 32.
8. Ibid., p. 32.
9. Ibid., p. 32. The first edition of *Story of a Soul* did not conceal the fact that Thérèse had doubts and went through a period of despondency. Later editions obscured this.
10. In 1893 Céline had received lessons from Edouard Krug, a pupil of Flandrin, who was willing to introduce her to the Salon.
11. DLTH, pp. 289–90.
12. Ms B 4r, OC, p. 228; TNT (1947), p. 205 (adapted). See also PN 34; OC, p. 717.
13. A selection of votive tablets from an immense number recorded by the author in the two locations cited. Countless chapels and churches contain similar tributes.
14. See also the account of the new portrait of Thérèse in *La Croix*, 31 August 1913. Another influence was *In the Cloister with Roses*, a painting of 1917 by Ferdinand Roybet, donated to Carmel in that year

by a Baroness Gérard; see *The Photo Album of St Thérèse of Lisieux*, commentary by F. de Sainte-Marie OCD; tr. P.-T. Rohrbach OCDP (New York, 1962).

15. Ms B 4v; OC, p. 228; TNT (1926), pp. 255–6.

16. The discovery that bones were the only mortal remains in Thérèse's grave fulfilled her prophecy – she told Céline: 'Little souls must find nothing to envy in me, so you can expect to find nothing but a skeleton'; see OM, p. 157. She also said that she would rather be 'reduced to powder' than be preserved like St Catherine of Bologna (see OC, p. 1029).

17. *Democratie* (3 October 1913), also quoted in GMC, pp. 56–7.

18. TNT (1947), p. 391.

19. See David Blackbourn, *The Marpingen Visions: Rationalism, Religion and the Rise of Modern Germany* (London, 1995), pp. 17–57, for an account of 'this golden age of organized mass pilgrimages'. The church '. . . aimed to dispose briskly of dubious apparitions and to construct a powerful official cult out of those it considered exemplary. The basilicas, organized pilgrimages, processions and confraternities served this purpose' (p. 57).

20. Cf. GMC, p. 107.

21. DE, OC, p. 1050.

22. LT 254; OC, pp. 609–10; Letters (S), p. 311.

23. DE with Marie Guérin; OC, p. 1183.

24. See, e.g., the tabular summaries in Pierre-André Sigal, *L'Homme et le Miracle dans la France Médiévale* (Paris, 1985), pp. 288–310.

25. TNT (1912), pp. 333–4.

26. 'To Scatter Flowers', OC, pp. 717–18; tr. R. and C. Winston in Ida Friederike Görres, *The Hidden Face: A Study of Thésèse of Lisieux* (London, 1959), p. 287.

27. TNT (1927), p. 431.

28. T, pp. 171–3.

29. Ibid., pp. 140–2.

30. Ibid., pp. 156–62.

31. Ibid., pp. 147–9.

32. Ibid., p. 180.

33. Ibid., p. 173.

34. TNT (1912), p. 388.

35. T, pp. 213–18.

36. William M. Cunningham, *The Unfolding of the Little Flower* (London, 1914), p. 130.

37. T, p. 135.

38. G, p. 199.

39. T, pp. 185–200.

40. TNT (1927), p. 399.

41. See, e.g., V. Sackville West, *The Eagle and The Dove* (London, 1943), pp. 172, 178–9.

42. T, pp. 166–71.
43. Jean-Marie Mayeur, 'Vie Réligieuse pendant la première Guerre', in *Histoire vécue du Peuple Chrétien*, ed. Jean Delumeau (Paris, 1979), vol. 2, p. 181.
44. Mgr Baudrillart in his preface to *La Vie Catholique dans la France contemporaine* (Paris, 1918).
45. See *Quelques Extraits des nombreuses lettres reçues au carmel de Lisieux pendant la guerre* (Lisieux, n.d.); J. Fontana, 'Attitude et sentiment du clergé et des catholiques devant et durant la guerre de 1914–1918' (Lille University III, thesis, 1973), *passim*; Annette Becker, *La Guerre et la Foi* (Paris, 1994), *passim*.
46. G, p. 177.
47. Ibid., pp. 168–70.
48. Ibid., pp. 173–5.
49. Ibid., p. 170.
50. Ibid., pp. 180–2.
51. TNT (1912), p. 354.
52. Ibid., p. 353.
53. Ibid., p. 355.
54. TNT (1947), p. 409.
55. OC, p. 1034.
56. NV, 16 July 1897; Görres, *The Hidden Face*, p. 341.
57. TNT (1947), p. 95.
58. DE, 17 July 1897; OC, p. 1050.

Bibliography

I: Works by Thérèse of Lisieux

Thérèse de l'Enfant-Jésus et de la Sainte-Face, *Œuvres complètes (Textes et Dernières Paroles)* (Paris, 2001).

Histoire d'une Âme (Lisieux, 1898).

Histoire d'une Âme, rev. edn (Lisieux, c.1915).

Histoire d'une Âme de Sainte Thérèse de Lisieux, ed. Conrad de Meester (Tournai, 1999).

A Little White Flower: The Story of Saint Thérèse of Lisieux, tr. Thomas N. Taylor (London, 1912).

A Little White Flower: The Story of Saint Thérèse of Lisieux, a revised translation of the definitive Carmelite edition of her autobiography by the Revd Thomas N. Taylor, witness before the tribunal of the Beatification (London, 1926).

Saint Thérèse of Lisieux, ed. and tr. T. N. Taylor (London, 1947).

Thérèse of Lisieux, Autobiography of a Saint, tr. Ronald Knox (London, 1958).

Story of a Soul, the Autobiography of St Thérèse of Lisieux, a new translation from the original manuscripts by John Clarke, OCD (Washington, DC, 1972).

La Bible avec Thérèse de Lisieux (Paris, 1997).

Collected Letters of Saint Thérèse de Lisieux, 1873–1897, ed. Abbé Combes, tr. F. J. Sheed (London, 1949).

Saint Thérèse of Lisieux, General Correspondence, tr. John Clarke, OCD, Vol. I (1877–90), Vol. II (1890–97) (Washington, DC, 1982).

Poems of Sr Teresa, Carmelite of Lisieux, tr. Susan L. Emery (London & Boston, 1907–8).

Poems of St Thérèse of the Child Jesus, tr. The Carmelites of Santa Clara (London, 1925).

Récréations Pieuses et Prières (Paris, 1992).

The Prayers of Saint Thérèse of Lisieux, tr. Alethia Kane, OCD (Washington, DC, 1997).

Novissima Verba (Lisieux, 1927).

Derniers Entretiens (Paris, 1971).

Positio super introductione Causae Bajocensis sue Lexoviensis Beatificationis et Canonizationis Servae Dei Sor. Theresiae . . . (Rome, 1914).

II: On Thérèse

Ahern, Patrick, *The Story of A Love: Maurice and Thérèse* (London, 1999).

Balthasar, Hans Urs von, *Two Sisters in the Spirit: Thérèse of Lisieux and Elizabeth of the Trinity* (San Francisco, 1992).

Chalon, Jean, *Thérèse de Lisieux* (Paris, 1991).

Cunningham, William M., *The Unfolding of the Little Flower* (London, 1914).

Day, Michael, *Christian Simplicity in St Thérèse* (London, 1953).

Delarue-Mardrus, Lucie, *Sainte Thérèse of Lisieux: a biography*, tr. H. Y. Chase (London, 1929).

Descouvemont, Pierre and Loose, Helmut Nils, *Thérèse et Lisieux* (Paris, 1991).

Furlong, Monica, *Thérèse of Lisieux* (London, 1987).

Geneviève, Soeur [Céline Martin], *Conseils et Souvenirs* (Paris, 1952).

Geneviève of the Holy Face, Sister, *A Memoir of my Sister Saint Thérèse*, tr. Carmelite Sisters of New York (Dublin, 1959).

Giloteaux, Abbé Paulin, *Saint Teresa of the Child Jesus; her supernatural character*, tr. William Reany, STL (London, 1928).

Görres, Ida Friederike, *The Hidden Face: A Study of St Thérèse of Lisieux*, tr. Richard and Clara Winston (London, 1959).

Gouley, B., Mauger, R. and Chevalier, E., *Sainte Thérèse de Lisieux* (Paris, 1997).

Maître, Jacques, *L'Orpheline de la Bérésina* (Paris, 1995).

Masson, Robert, *Souffrance des Hommes* (Saint-Paul, 1997).

Mauriac, François, *Bloc-Notes*, Vols. 1–5 (Paris, 1958–71).

Mauriac, François, *Nouveaux Mémoires Intérieurs* (Paris, 1965).

Meersch, Maxence van der, *La Petite Sainte Thérèse* (Paris, 1947).

Meester, Conrad de, *Les mains vides. Un message de Thérèse* (Paris, 1972).

O'Mahony, Christopher, ed. and tr., *St Thérèse of Lisieux by those who knew her. Testimonies from the process of beatification* (Dublin, 1975).

Piat, Stéphane-Joseph, OFM, *The Story of A Family*, tr. a Benedictine of Stanbrook Abbey (Dublin, 1947).

Piat, Stéphane-Joseph, OFM, *Léonie: Une sœur de Sainte Thérèse à la Visitation* (Lisieux, 1966).

Redmond, Paulinus, *Louis and Zélie Martin, The seed and the root of the Little Flower* (London, 1995).

Sackville West, Victoria, *The Eagle and The Dove* (London, 1943).

Sainte-Marie, F. de, OCD (ed.), *The Photo Album of St Thérèse of Lisieux*, tr. P.-T. Rohrbach, OCDP (New York, 1962).

Six, Jean-François, *La véritable enfance de Thérèse de Lisieux: Névrose et Sainteté* (Paris, 1972).

Six, Jean-François, *Lumière de la nuit: les 18 derniers mois de Thérèse de Lisieux* (Paris, 1995).

Six, Jean-François, *Thérèse de Lisieux: son combat spirituel sa voie* (Paris, 1998).

Teil, Roger de Basevi, *The Cause of Beatification of the Little Flower of Jesus* (London, 1913).

Viquesnel, Jacques, *Promenades en Normandie avec Sainte Thérèse de Lisieux* (Condée-sur-Noireau, 1993).

III: Other works

Details of other works cited in the book are given in the relevant endnotes.